PENGUIN CANADA

JUST BECAUSE IT'S NOT WRONG
DOESN'T MAKE IT RIGHT

BARBARA COLOROSO is an internationally recognized speaker and author in the areas of parenting, teaching, school discipline, nonviolent conflict resolution, reconciliatory justice, and grieving. Her bestselling books include *Parenting through Crisis*; *The Bully, the Bullied, and the Bystander*; and *kids are worth it!*

Also by Barbara Coloroso

kids are worth it!

Parenting through Crisis

Parenting Wit and Wisdom from Barbara Coloroso

The Bully, the Bullied, and the Bystander

Barbara Coloroso

Just because it's not wrong doesn't make it right

From toddlers to teens, teaching kids to think and act ethically

PENGUIN
CANADA

PENGUIN CANADA

Published by the Penguin Group

Penguin Group (Canada), 90 Eglinton Avenue East, Suite 700, Toronto, Ontario, Canada
M4P 2Y3 (a division of Pearson Canada Inc.)

Penguin Group (USA) Inc., 375 Hudson Street, New York, New York 10014, U.S.A.
Penguin Books Ltd, 80 Strand, London WC2R 0RL, England
Penguin Ireland, 25 St Stephen's Green, Dublin 2, Ireland (a division of Penguin Books Ltd)
Penguin Group (Australia), 250 Camberwell Road, Camberwell, Victoria 3124, Australia
(a division of Pearson Australia Group Pty Ltd)
Penguin Books India Pvt Ltd, 11 Community Centre, Panchsheel Park, New Delhi – 110 017,
India
Penguin Group (NZ), cnr Airborne and Rosedale Roads, Albany, Auckland 1310, New Zealand
(a division of Pearson New Zealand Ltd)
Penguin Books (South Africa) (Pty) Ltd, 24 Sturdee Avenue, Rosebank, Johannesburg 2196,
South Africa

Penguin Books Ltd, Registered Offices: 80 Strand, London WC2R 0RL, England

First published in a Viking Canada hardcover by Penguin Group (Canada),
a division of Pearson Canada Inc., 2005
Published in this edition, 2007

1 2 3 4 5 6 7 8 9 10 (WEB)

Copyright © Barbara Coloroso, 2005

The Internet Safety Tips are reprinted with permission from the *Elementary Safety
Book for Children*, published by Regional Maple Leaf Communications, Inc.

Excerpt from "Don't Laugh at Me," copyright © 1998 Sony/ATV Tunes L.L.C.,
David Aaron Music and Built on Rock Music. All rights on behalf of Sony/ATV Tunes L.L.C.
and David Aaron Music administered by Sony/ATV Music Publishing, 8 Music Square West,
Nashville, TN 372032. All rights reserved. Used by permission.

Manufactured in Canada.

ISBN-10: 0-14-301609-1
ISBN-13: 978-0-14-301609-0

Library and Archives Canada Cataloguing in Publication data available upon request

Visit the Penguin Group (Canada) website at **www.penguin.ca**

Special and corporate bulk purchase rates available; please see
www.penguin.ca/corporatesales or call 1-800-810-3104, ext. 477 or 474

To Cynthia Good, who cared that this book be written
and entrusted me with the project.

For Stephen Lewis and the Stephen Lewis Foundation
(www.stephenlewisfoundation.org). You put a face
on the suffering in Africa, making it nigh
to impossible to turn a blind eye.

Otto Frank took a deep breath and asked, "Miep, are you willing to take on the responsibility of taking care of us while we are in hiding?"

"Of course," I answered.

There is a look between two people once or twice in a lifetime that cannot be described by words. That look passed between us.... I am not a hero.... I was only willing to do what was asked of me and what seemed necessary at the time.

—FROM THE EXHIBIT *ANNE FRANK: A HISTORY FOR TODAY* (ANNE FRANK CENTER USA)

Contents

A Cautionary Tale

I met him in Kigali, the capital of Rwanda, on my first full day in the city. Jean Paul, a tall, quiet twenty-one-year-old with a shy smile and piercing eyes, refused to go into the National Genocide Memorial Museum with us. Instead, at the gateway arch of the complex he stood as a lone sentry, guarding simultaneously the graveyard in front of him and the hauntingly beautiful hills behind.

In 1994 he fled alone into those hills as a scared, orphaned eleven-year-old. He had no need to view the pictures that covered the walls of this huge building; he had enough etched in his own mind. He didn't need to walk the paths between the thousands of graves; he had stumbled over plenty of dead bodies in those hills. He didn't need to see the rows of skulls of babies, toddlers, and eleven-year-olds each bearing the marks of the machetes that killed them; he had four machete scars on his own head. He didn't need to see the blood-soaked clothes and shoes piled high in the corner; his own clothes were soaked with the blood of his parents and two sisters. Before fleeing from the church in Nyarubuye, he stood frozen in fear as he watched the murderers finish their "work" of "killing the cockroaches" with machetes and *masu*—nail-studded clubs.

In April of 1994, the Hutu government of Rwanda called upon the Hutu majority to kill everyone in the Tutsi minority. In one hundred days almost one million men, women, and children were murdered by their neighbors, schoolmates, colleagues, relatives, and supposed friends. An estimated 400,000 of the dead were children and 95,000 more were orphaned.

It was not hostility that fueled this genocide. Herbert Kellman, who has studied evil and violence, suggests, "We can learn more by looking, not at the motives for violence, but at the conditions under which the usual moral inhibitions against violence can be weakened." These include:

1. unquestioning obedience to authority that relieved the killers of their personal responsibility;
2. routinization that turned the commission of violence into a normal operation; and
3. dehumanization, in which the Tutsis were stripped of their humanity, their personal identity, and any connection to the community.

Couple these with the sense of entitlement, the liberty to exclude, and the intolerance toward differences that became entrenched during the colonization period and the dictatorship that followed, and you have a recipe for a genocide.

By studying the conditions under which ordinary people can commit extraordinary evil, is it possible to create conditions in our home, our schools, and our communities that will strengthen inhibitions against violence and nurture those bonds that connect us one to another? Can we use these bonds to nourish a deep passion to alleviate another's pain and sorrow? To ask "What are you going through?" and "What do you need?"? I think we can.

Adopted after the genocide by a man and a woman who themselves had fled into those same hills during the killing, Jean Paul has nightmares now only in April.

> People can be made bad, and they can be taught to be good.
>
> —PRESIDENT PAUL KAGAME, WHO AS GENERAL OF THE RWANDAN PATRIOTIC FRONT (RPF) LED HIS WELL-DISCIPLINED, RAGTAG ARMY INTO RWANDA AND DID SOMETHING THE INTERNATIONAL COMMUNITY HAD FAILED TO DO ONE HUNDRED DAYS BEFORE—STOPPED THE GENOCIDE

Introduction:
It Is in Us to Care

Ethic: A basic human moral attitude.
Ethics: A philosophical or theological theory of moral attitudes, values, and norms.

It is an *ethic* rooted in deep caring, not the study of *ethics*, that is the concern of this book. Studying the various theories of morality can be an interesting and mind-boggling exercise, and at the end we might know even less about how to raise a child who can think and act ethically than we did before we began. What we would know is that there are many contradictory theories, and almost as many different systems of morality.

We could compare Immanuel Kant's theories to Pete Singer's, or universalism to utilitarianism, or absolutism to relativism. We could memorize the cardinal virtues, the theological virtues, the classic Greek virtues and values; add to them civil liberties, humanistic values, mystical values, ideals, the basic complement of instinctual states, behavioral tie-ins with conditioning theories, the vices of excess virtue, vices of defect (absence of virtue), and violence viewed as excessive defect. Disregarding all of the above, we could turn instead to a popular character education program, or grab a book of virtues that lists the fifty-six vital virtues our children need to work on during a year.

When finished, we would still have to ask:

"Do we emphasize the virtues of liberty and autonomy, or loyalty and respect for authority?"

"Do we value justice over mercy?"

"Do we inculcate children with 'traditional' values; or do we show them how to adhere to and practice certain virtues and avoid certain vices; or do we teach them to follow certain absolute rules or dogma—with the possibility of rejecting people who don't adhere to those rules or don't believe the dogma?"

"What happens when two virtues clash or contradict one another?"

"What is the difference between an ethical dilemma and an ethical temptation?"

And finally, "What is a moral child?" and "Do we want to raise a moral child? If so, how do we do it? If not, why not? Is there an alternative?"

Just Because It's Not Wrong Doesn't Make It Right is about something much simpler, though not necessarily easier. It is about a way of being in the world, about an ethic connected so deeply and pervasively to the whole of our humanity that there is no need to impose it, regulate it, or enforce it. I am heartened that people throughout the world—parents, educators, religious leaders, sociologists, theologians, and philosophers—are speaking out about the dangers of rigid moral absolutism, moral relativism, and nihilism. It is in us to care. We are as capable of being good as we are of doing harm.

If we are to raise kids who can think and act ethically, we don't begin with the thinking or the acting. We begin with *caring*—caring for our children and nurturing their innate ability to care; helping them to see themselves as both lovable and loving. Such an ethic is primarily about relationships, not principles or virtues or values. It is not that principles, virtues, and values have no purpose. They do. In an ethic rooted in deep caring, they are *in service to* and *at the service of that caring*. When children know that they are cared for, then they can begin caring deeply, sharing generously, and helping willingly. In turn, these three serve as strong antidotes to hating, hoarding, and harming—the three virulent agents that can rip apart the fabric of human relationships.

In *kids are worth it! Giving Your Child the Gift of Inner Discipline*, I offered practical advice for parents of toddlers through teenagers on how to use the stuff of everyday family life—chores, mealtime, sibling rivalry, toilet training, bedtime, and allowances—to create a home environment in which kids can become self-disciplined, responsible, resourceful, resilient human beings capable of acting in their own best interests, standing up for themselves, and exercising their own rights while respecting the rights and legitimate needs of others. Knowing how to think, not just what to think; feeling empowered, not controlled or manipulated; being able to distinguish between realities that must be accepted and problems that can be solved; and being able to act with civility and integrity—these are lessons that can be learned through these everyday and at times mundane activities. These same activities can provide opportunities to teach children to think and act ethically.

The tools of good parenting—acting with integrity, civility, and compassion; walking your talk and talking your walk; treating kids with respect; giving them a sense of positive power in their own lives; giving them opportunities to make decisions, take responsibility for their actions, and learn from their successes and mistakes—are the same parenting tools you can use to help create an environment that is conducive to raising children who care deeply, share generously, and help willingly; who can stand up for another child and against an injustice when the burden is heavy; and who can do the right thing simply because it is the right thing to do.

This book is an attempt to delve more deeply into this way of being in the world, and into this human wisdom that enables us to meet one another morally.

Concerned with the social forces that "make human beings human," internationally renowned authority on child development Dr. Urie Bronfenbrenner warned of the breakdown of the social support system that had once helped children to thrive. "We've got all kinds of forces that are interfering and blocking the process of civilizing human beings and making them competent and responsible," he told the *Syracuse Post-Standard* in 1996. Since our story about our human nature in today's social and cultural climate is part and parcel of our human nature *and* our social and cultural climate, part of raising kids who can think and act ethically involves looking for ways of being in the world that will reduce the harm we do to one another and to our planet. At the same time, it involves creating homes, schools, and communities that will effectively support us in raising our kids. Our story is also guided by our compassion and loving-kindness, which recognizes that there is no "I" without a "Thou," no "We" without community, and no way to survive without honoring both our unique individuality and our common humanity.

BARBARA COLOROSO
SEPTEMBER 2005

Chapter 1

An Ethic Rooted in Deep Caring

The first step in the evolution of ethics is a sense of solidarity with other human beings.
—ALBERT SCHWEITZER

Sixteen-year-old Anita regularly visited an elderly neighbor, running errands for her and listening to her stories, "because Ms. Dean lives alone and has no grandkids to visit her."

In her playgroup four-year-old Melissa happily shared her chocolate chip cookie with a boy who had left his own snack at home. When asked why she shared, she replied, "Because he was hungry."

Seven-year-old Marcus helped his classmate complete a math assignment, "because he needed help."

None of these kids said, "I need to visit an elderly person for my community service credits"; "I get points in the character education program this week if I am caught sharing. Besides, the other boy might give me part of his cookie tomorrow"; "I want to get Helper of the Week." Each one of them not only felt a solidarity with the other person, they saw a person in need and responded to that person with deep caring. There was no reliance on principles, no acting on sheer emotions, no complicated philosophy or dogma. There was no should or ought; no rule demanding that they be kind, share a cookie, or help a classmate; and no external bribe to induce and no reward to compensate. They were simply reaching out in compassion and/or loving-kindness to another person.

THE "I AND THOU" AND "WE": THE RELATIONSHIP OF CARING

> Injustice anywhere is a threat to justice everywhere.
> We are caught in an inescapable network of mutuality,
> tied to a single garment of destiny.
> —MARTIN LUTHER KING, JR.
> *LETTERS FROM A BIRMINGHAM JAIL*

An ethic that is rooted in deep caring is primarily about such reaching out and the relationship that is thus created. Martin Buber called these encounters "meeting one another as an I and a Thou." To see another as a "Thou" is to honor our uniqueness and our individuality, and at the same time to recognize our common bond, our solidarity and interdependence. What seems a paradox is actually two necessary parts of the whole: our individuality and our commonality. We are both an "I and a Thou" and a "We." Putting it in mathematical terms, Arthur Eddington explained, "We used to think that if we knew one, we knew two, because one and one are two. We are learning that we must learn a great deal about 'and.'"

It is in the "and" that our basic moral attitude—i.e., our ethic—exists. When we care deeply, share generously, and help willingly, we do it in the context of the "I and Thou" in the now. When we hate, hoard, or harm, we violate, denigrate, or diminish not only the "I and Thou" but also the "We." Explaining the African concept of *ubuntu*, Archbishop Desmond Tutu noted that it means "I am me only because you are you; my humanity is caught up in your humanity. If I dehumanize you, I am inexorably dehumanized.... [C]oncern for others is the best form of self-interest." Each one of us depends on the well-being of the whole; if the "We" is diminished, each one of us is less.

An ethic rooted merely in principles, rules, or dogma attempts the development of the *virtuous person*, not the nurturing of *moral relationships*. Principles tend to speak to the "I," the individual, alone: "Be loyal, be truthful, be trustworthy, be kind, be civil, be responsible." Rules also tend to speak to the "I": "Don't lie, don't cheat, don't steal." Dogma has the tendency to label acts done by the individual as sins or virtues based solely on the individual and not on the potential social consequences of those acts. Commenting on unquestioning obedience to dogma in regard to laws and church teachings concerning slavery, Mark Twain wrote: "Loyalty to petrified opinion never yet broke a chain or freed a human soul." All three—principles, rules, and dogma—can contribute to the breaking down of "We" into an "Us" and a "Them," good people versus bad people, the saved and the damned.

> What the world needs now, respects now, demands now, understands now … is generous justice, reckless love, and limitless listening.
> —SISTER JOAN CHITTISTER, *FIRE IN THESE ASHES: A SPIRITUALITY OF CONTEMPORARY RELIGIOUS LIFE*

LOOKING BEYOND THE RULES

It is a proud ethic with a humble and wary heart.
—NEL NODDING, *CARING, A FEMININE*
APPROACH TO ETHICS AND MORAL EDUCATION

The children who reached out to their peers in the examples given earlier did so without considering a complicated philosophy or dogma. There was no *should* or *ought*, no rule demanding that they be kind, share a cookie, or help a classmate. They were simply reaching out to another person.

Principles, rules, and dogma can be used for good or for ill. They can help prevent ethical abuses, or they can serve as the excuse for them. It is possible to be truthful in a mean-spirited way ("You look ugly in that outfit." "What a gross hairdo."). It is possible for a lie to be a greater good than the truth, to be a "virtue," not a "vice." Sol Frenkel fled from his native Poland, where Nazi pogroms wiped out everyone else in his immediate family. Mr. Frenkel escaped only because of forged work papers that identified him as a Gentile, papers that were acquired through lying, cheating, and stealing. His forgeries saved not only his life, but the lives of at least twenty other people.

It is possible to follow the narrow letter of the law or rule and at the same time violate its spirit. A teen at a Georgia high school was punished for not hanging up his cellphone. He was spotted by a teacher who, citing a district policy against cellphone use during school hours, told him to end the call right away. The boy told the teacher, "I'm on the phone with my mom in Iraq. I am not going to give you the phone." An altercation ensued when the teacher took the phone from him, and the boy was suspended for ten days. The altercation could have been avoided if the teacher had been willing to meet the young boy with deep caring and not as a mere rule-enforcer. The school district's rule was designed to "preserve instructional time and decorum in the schools." Deep caring would have trumped the rule once the teacher knew that it was a once-a-month phone call from the boy's mother. Listening and being present to the boy's anguish could have created a very different outcome.

G. K. Chesterton wrote of the problem with ironclad tenets: "Dogma does not mean the absence of thought, but the end of thought." In Brielle, New Jersey, an eight-year-old girl, who suffers from celiac sprue disease and thus cannot eat wheat, had her Catholic first communion declared invalid by the bishop of the diocese because the host that was used was a rice wafer and did not contain the required unleavened bread. Church doctrine states that, in keeping with the bread served at the Last Supper, communion wafers must have the unleavened wheat. Never mind that for the young girl the consequence of eating a wheat host could be death. The bishop of Trenton said in a statement: "This is not an issue to be determined at the diocesan or parish level, but has already been decided for the Roman Catholic Church throughout the world by Vatican authority." The end of thought. The priest who gave her the rice substitute was acting out of deep caring for the little girl and in the spirit of communion.

Navy helicopter pilots were reprimanded by their commanding officer after they diverted their mission of delivering supplies to a naval station and instead rescued over one hundred people from their rooftops after Hurricane

Katrina hit New Orleans in the summer of 2005. Their commanding officer told the pilots that "helping civilians was laudable" but that it was an "unacceptable diversion from their main mission of delivering supplies." The people rescued would beg to differ. In their passion to alleviate the pain of others, the Navy helicopter pilots put aside the order and reached out to those desperate people, answering in action the questions "What are you going through?" "What do you need?" and "What can I do?" After the reprimand, some members of the unit stopped wearing the search-and-rescue patch on their sleeves that read "So Others May Live."

After getting arrested for marching in protest, British campaigner for women's suffrage Emmeline Pankhurst declared, "We have taken this action, because as women we realize that the condition of our sex is so deplorable that it is our duty even to break the law in order to call attention to the reasons why we do so." She was willing to break an unjust law and accept the consequences of jail in order to help create a more just, fair, and equitable society.

A rigid adherence to rules, principles, and dogmas— moral absolutism—requires an *always* and a *never*. Always tell the truth; no cellphone use in school must always be enforced; you must, without question, always obey a lawful order, even in the face of human desperation; if the Church says only a wheat host will do, then only a wheat host will do, always. Never lie; never contravene a rule or an edict; never disobey an order or violate a law. Those who adhere to moral absolutism—who question any bending of any of the principles, rules, or dogma—often fear that to bend at all is to head down a slippery slope to a place where no principles are held, no rules apply, no orders are obeyed, and no dogma is embraced—in other words, moral relativism.

I am not espousing a sort of "middle mush" here, not a dash of absolutism added to a stew of relativism, or vice versa. I am also not suggesting that there be any *bend* in the principles, rules, or dogma. Once bending begins, principles, rules, or dogma can be bent beyond recognition, stretched beyond usefulness. Once exceptions are admitted and encoded, they can be used to justify any number of negative acts, including violence against those who are different from us: "Thou shalt not kill, *except or unless* ..." United States Supreme Court Justice Thurgood Marshall alluded to the way in which our rules can evolve and serve different ends when he wrote, "What is striking is the role legal principles have played throughout America's history in determining the condition of Negroes. They were enslaved by law, emancipated by law, disenfranchised and segregated by law; and finally, they have begun to win equality by law."

In an ethic rooted in deep caring, the relationship comes first; principles, rules, and dogma are *at the service of* that caring. There is no bending. The principle is held to be a good one; it just might not be the one that is called into the service of deep caring in the *now*. Sometimes, principles, rules, and dogma must be *set aside* in order not to hinder compassion and loving-kindness, the two complimentary qualities of deep caring. Knowing when to set aside principles, rules, or dogma involves using our heart, our head, and our messy emotions and instincts.

COMPASSION AND LOVING-KINDNESS

Compassion and loving kindness complement each
other. They are the antidotes to selfish desire, hatred
and cruelty.

—ANTHONY FLANAGAN

In the beginning of this book I quoted Miep Gies, the
woman who hid and cared for the Otto Frank family during
World War II. When asked why she was willing to take on
such a responsibility, she said, "There is a look between two
people once or twice in a lifetime that cannot be described
by words. That look passed between us.... I am not a hero. I
was only willing to do what was asked of me and what
seemed necessary at the time." For Miep, to act was a *must*.
And her actions throughout the time she hid the family
embodied both compassion and loving-kindness.

Compassion is the sympathetic consciousness of
another's sorrow, pain, or misery, together with the deep
passion and desire to alleviate it. This deep passion is more
than a sentiment or a thought. It is our heart, our head, our
senses, and our body joined in an effort to alleviate the pain
and suffering of the "Thou." We can't be truly compassionate by merely sitting back, watching the misery, and
commenting, "Oh, how awful." Nor are we compassionate
when we express our sorrow or concern and say, "I'm so
sorry that happened," and then do nothing. Compassion is
knowing, feeling, and being compelled to do something to
alleviate another's misery.

Writer and theologian Matthew Fox said, "Compassion is
not sentiment, but making justice and doing works of

mercy." Without the actions of "making justice and doing works of mercy" we remain merely agitated, sorrowful, or concerned. Compassion implies a *must* that compels us to do something to help alleviate the sorrow, pain, or misery of the other. There is no compassion without action, even if that action is simply being completely present in mind and heart and body to one who is suffering when no other action is possible. Thomas Merton described compassion as "the keen awareness of the interdependence of all things." To act compassionately is to connect "I" and "Thou."

Loving-kindness is the desire to extend care, consideration, and goodwill to each and every one we meet. Nursing student Joann C. Jones wrote a note about a professor who gave the second-year nursing students a quiz. The last question on the exam was "What is the first name of the woman who cleans the school?" One student asked if the last question would count toward the grade. The professor answered, "Absolutely. In your careers, you will meet many people. All are significant. They deserve your attention and care, even if all you do is smile and say hello." Joann, who had met the cleaning woman several times, handed in her paper with that last question blank. She ended her note by saying, "I've never forgotten that lesson. I also learned her name was Dorothy."

Teaching children that each and every person they meet is significant and needs to be treated with loving-kindness is more than teaching them to have manners, although manners do matter. It is more than teaching them how to say please and thank you, although those count, too. It is teaching them first that *they* matter, that they have dignity and worth simply because they are "totally unique," as anthropologist Margaret Mead said, "just like everyone else." If we are to help them become lovable and loving human beings, we need to provide them with a secure, safe, nurturing environment—offering them unconditional love, caring touch, tenderness, and concern for their physical, emotional, and spiritual well-being. It is within such an environment that they can begin to make choices, decisions, and mistakes, to assume responsibilities and become actively involved family members. Engaging children in critical reflection, teaching them to be aware always of the potential consequences (intended and unintended) of their words and deeds, showing them how to take responsibility for their actions and inactions, their accomplishments and their mistakes—all this can empower them to reach out to others, to join with others in cooperative and collaborative adventures, and to develop strong friendships. It is teaching them ways and whys of sharing and caring and helping and serving, and giving them the opportunities to do all four.

In 1993, Professor Chuck Wall walked into his classroom at Bakersfield College and gave his eighteen students the week's assignment: "Today, I will commit one random act of senseless kindness." The students were thoroughly energized by their individual projects and shortly after began their own campaign, with bumper stickers that read "Today, I will commit one random act of senseless KINDNESS ... Will you?" It was the beginning of what would become an international "Random Acts of Kindness" project.

Too often we underestimate the power of a touch, a smile, a kind word, a listening ear, an honest compli-

ment, or the smallest act of caring, all of which have
the potential to turn a life around.

—LEO BUSCAGLIA, *LIVING, LOVING AND LEARNING*

EMPATHY AND SYMPATHY

If I would have known what troubles you were bearing
I would have been more gentle, more caring, and tried
to give you gladness for a space.

—MARY CAROLYN DAVIES

Compassion and loving-kindness are at once both the
impetus for and the expression of our thinking and acting
ethically. The driving forces behind compassion and loving-
kindness are **empathy** and **sympathy**.

Empathy and sympathy are often mistakenly spoken of as
if they were one and the same. And there are many conflicting definitions of the two words. Some writers define them
as synonymous, while others say that "empathy" is the new
term that is simply replacing "sympathy." And some reverse
the definitions.

For the purposes of this book, I use the word "empathy"
to imply resonance, "sympathy" to imply responsiveness.
When we empathize we *resonate* with another, we echo or
amplify that person's feelings. When we sympathize we
respond to another, and our feelings are in harmony with the
other's, but not the same. Both empathy and sympathy are
critical to human bonding.

If a child sees another child who is happy, she feels that
happiness herself—an experience of empathy. This "emotional
contagion" called mimicry is a basic biological mechanism

that causes us, from infancy on, to imitate the facial expressions, postures, and voices of people around us. Notice how a yawn is contagious. Even very young babies smile when someone smiles at them. And how can one resist the smile of a baby (perhaps nature's way of inviting an empathic response from caregivers)?

If a child sees someone in distress, she, too, feels that distress vicariously. Empathy appears to have its roots in the empathic stress present in newborns. Infants become distressed when near someone in distress. In a sense, they echo or resonate with the other person's feelings. For children, it is the beginning of their knowing that we are all made of the same delicate fabric. A common expression today is "I feel your pain." Feeling the happiness or the pain of another helps create the sense of "We."

As children develop their intellectual skills and expand their emotional repertoire to include a wider range of emotional expressions, they become increasingly able to "walk in another's shoes." In empathy, this walk means "I imagine how *I* would feel in *her* shoes." In his essay "When Compassion Becomes Dissent," David James Duncan describes the impact of this experience:

> *What would it be to be like that black girl four rows in front of me?* A little white girl wonders in school one morning. Her imagination sets to work, creating unwritten fiction. In her mind she becomes the black girl, dons her clothes, accent, skin, joins her friends after school, goes home to her family, lives that life. No firsthand experience is taking place. Nothing newsworthy is happening. Yet a white-

girl-turned-fictitiously-black is linking skin hue to life, skin hue to choice of friends and neighborhood, skin hue to opportunity and history. Words she used without thinking—*African, color, white*—feel suddenly different. And when her imaginary game is over they'll still sound different. Via sheer fiction, empathy enters a human heart.

This experience of perspective-taking (imagining what others see, think, or feel) can enhance a child's empathic reaction, and thus can increase the chances that she will act prosocially toward the girl whose shoes she has figuratively walked in. That "fellow feeling," being tuned in to another, can propel a child to perform acts of loving-kindness or compassion, seeing the other as part of the "We." Scientist and educator George Washington Carver wrote of our collective "We": "How far you go in life depends on your being tender with the young, compassionate with the aged, sympathetic with the striving and tolerant of the weak and the strong. Because someday in life you will have been all of these."

It is possible for empathy to be corrupted, perverted, or negated. Children who bully often have empathy, in the sense that they are able to vicariously experience the targeted child's feelings and take great glee in causing further distress. They can imagine how the other child feels in his own shoes and take great pleasure in the thought. Con artists can empathize with the plight of others, and still take off with all of their money.

Rationalizing that the people in distress brought their problems on themselves, or that they somehow deserve the misery, or that they are "not like us" can negate empathy. (We kill "vermin," "cockroaches," "enemies"—not flesh-and-blood humans who laugh and cry like we do, who have the same values we do.)

Sympathy is most commonly understood as a sorrow or concern in response to someone else's distress or misery. A child who has sympathy for another child is responsive to the other child's pain, but her own feelings are different from the feelings of the child in pain. This sorrow or concern can help to propel a child to do something to relieve the other's pain, "because he was hungry." In essence, one child has taken another child's pain into herself and responded, not with an identical feeling, but with one that is helpful. Empathy helps create the sense of "We" through feelings in common; sympathy helps create the sense of "I and Thou" through two unique feelings, each bound to the other by the "and." The more children can do both—resonate and respond—the better able they will be to call upon either or both to care deeply, share generously, and help willingly.

Walking in someone else's shoes comes into play with sympathy as well as empathy. Once a child imagines not how *he* would feel in *her* shoes, but how *she* feels in *her own* shoes, he can receive that feeling into himself and respond. Sympathy will likely lead him to a different kind of action than would have come into play if he resonated with the girl's feelings. With empathy, resonating with the girl's feelings, he might shudder and say, "I would feel awful," or "She must feel awful," and decide he will do everything possible to avoid ever getting into those shoes. He might also decide he will do whatever it takes to help her out of that situation.

He feels bad because she feels bad, and he wants to make the bad feeling go away for both of them. With sympathy, his feelings don't resonate, they respond. He takes into himself her feelings and, with concern for her well-being, does something to comfort her or relieve her suffering.

In sympathy the direction of the caring is toward the other, the "Thou." This does not mean that the "I" won't benefit in some way from the action; it is just that the intention is first and foremost to relieve the other's suffering. In sympathy, you are more likely to better grasp what the other needs to relieve the suffering because you are *responding* to their pain, not simply *resonating* with it. Resonating leaves the possibility of getting caught up in what would be relief for *you* instead of what would be relief for *her*.

None of us wants empathy from the lawyer who is handling our case, especially if we are feeling like basket-cases ourselves. What we need is someone who is *receptive* to our frayed nerves, our disjointed sentences, our disorganized files, and *responds* with concern and competence. And at $150 an hour, we probably don't want to hear that she feels our pain because she has been through this herself. Or maybe we do. Then, what we will hopefully get is both empathy *and* sympathy. When we make a 911 call, we hope for sympathy and not empathy on the other end. What we need is someone who will receive our pain and respond with something more helpful than a mirror image of our own panic. And sometimes what we all want is someone to just listen to our story and not be so quick to have him or her tells us his or hers—to listen and be present.

Empathy does not always produce a connecting response. It is possible to have empathy for someone—to know what they are feeling and know it deeply—but have no energy or inclination to reach out to them, because you are so emotionally drained yourself. It might take too much energy and pain to be open to receive another's feelings and then take the next step and respond. Instead you are both alone in your own sea of grief. It is not uncommon for a man and a woman to love one another deeply and yet not respond compassionately to each other after the death of their child. They both can walk in the other's shoes and even resonate with the other's grief, but not have the desire or energy to reach out with compassion in an attempt to relieve the other's pain. This is the time they both need community—others to reach out and embrace each one.

Sympathy can be used in the service of loving-kindness as well as in the service of compassion. We can be sympathetic to another's cause without feeling the same passion they do for it. A parent of teenagers can sympathize with a group of young moms who want to start a co-op for their toddlers. She feels their energy and excitement, and she responds—not with the same energy and excitement (she's glad to be beyond that stage in parenting) but with an offer to help them organize the group.

Sympathy can be as easily corrupted as empathy, and it has gotten a bad rap since the term empathy came into use in the late 1800s and rose to prominence in the early 1900s. Sympathy is not merely feeling sorry or upset about someone else's plight. It is a much greater regard, a deep sorrow and/or concern for the weal and woe of the other.

Sympathy is often labeled as sappy, sentimental, or patronizing. It is none of these when it is a sincere response to another person's pain. Perverted or corrupted, it can be all three. When a person wants to *appear* sympathetic but is not really open to taking in the other person's distress, his reaction—not *response*—will tend to be artificial, sappy, sentimental, and/or patronizing. With flowery words and a condescending tone, the impostor talks a good talk but has no intention of relieving the other person's pain. Such a "show of sympathy" is merely an act of self-indulgence. A politician hugging disaster victims for a photo op and then doing none of the things in his power to help those in dire straits is the embodiment of sympathy corrupted.

The same rationalizations that negated empathy can negate sympathy—he brought the problems on himself; he deserved it; she's "not like us." Sympathy can be overwhelmed, especially when the trauma or tragedy is so devastating that the one who is sympathetic begins to feel helpless and hopeless. Sympathy can also be overwhelmed by anger. When a teenager does something irresponsible, is injured, and has harmed someone else, sympathy for him can be overwhelmed by the frustration and anger we feel because of the stupidity of the act and the hurt inflicted on an innocent party. Sympathy can be drowned out by a clamor for revenge, and totally deadened by hate.

Tears without action are wasted sentiment.
—JODI WILLIAMS, NOBEL LAUREATE

THE GOLDEN RULE AND ANOTHER POSSIBILITY

The highest wisdom is kindness.
—THE TALMUD

The ethic that we should treat others as we ourselves want to be treated, and not in a way we ourselves would not want to be treated, is found in all the great religions of the world. These tenets are in line with empathy—they call on us to resonate, to echo or amplify the feelings of others. However, there are times when it is best that we *not* do for another what we would want done for ourselves. The other, as a unique individual in a unique situation, might ask of us a different response than the one we would desire for ourselves. In *Parenting Through Crisis* I wrote about a young boy dying of cancer who decided he did not want to continue treatment and wanted to spend his final days without the drugs that made him so groggy and nauseated. In loving-kindness and deep compassion, his grief-stricken parents honored his choice. It is sympathy, more than empathy, that allows us to go in this direction. Sympathy responds to "What are you going through, what do you need, what can I do to help?" There are times when it is our *common humanity* that must be considered; at other times it is our *uniqueness* and the *uniqueness of the other* that are front and center. And sometimes it is both. What may be good for one of us may be a disaster for all of us. Deep caring requires that we discern the difference. It is our head, our heart, and our emotions and instincts that are a help or hindrance in discerning that difference.

> We don't set out to save the world; we set out to wonder how other people are doing and to reflect on how our actions affect other people's hearts.
> —PEMA CHODRON, *WHEN THINGS FALL APART*

THE HEAD, THE HEART, AND THOSE MESSY EMOTIONS AND INSTINCTS

And if he were really to do good, he would have needed, in addition to principles, a heart capable of violating them—a heart which knows only of the particular, not of the general case, and which achieves greatness in little actions.
—BORIS PASTERNAK, *DOCTOR ZHIVAGO*

A T-shirt caught my attention. The writing on the front asked the question, "What is the difference between ignorance and apathy?" The back of the shirt had the answer: "I don't know and I don't care." Philosophers and theologians have written volumes on the distinction between the role of the mind and the role of the heart in learning to think and act ethically. That T-shirt said it in fifteen words. To be ignorant of how to behave ethically is one thing; to not care is wholly another. And the development of both the mind *(knowing)* and the heart *(caring)* is critical to raising children who can think and act ethically.

Jason was visibly upset as he ran to his mother: "Olivia has a nosebleed and I can't make it stop" *(I don't know how)*. Another child saw Olivia, shrugged her shoulders, and said, "I'm not touching her. Someone else can handle the bloody mess" *(I don't care)*.

When asked why he wasn't voting in the upcoming national election, one university student interviewed by a staff reporter at *USA Today* summed up his own apathy and ignorance in one sentence: "I don't care enough to care about why I don't care."

The mind is the home of the intellect; the heart is the center of deep caring (compassion and loving-kindness). And working with the mind and the heart are our emotions and instincts. Emotions are feelings, which in turn create moods, which in turn create temperaments. Instincts are the primal forces that produce mimicry, empathic distress, and the *fright, flight, or fight* response. All four interact with one another, and in turn are influenced by and interact with the cultural and social environment. And although they are clearly separate here for the purpose of discussion, in real life they are constantly changing, and causing change, and are not always so easy to separate.

HEAD

> Knowledge alone is not enough. It must be leavened
> with magnanimity before it becomes wisdom.
> —ADLAI STEVENSON

Simply knowing laws, precepts, and rules is no guarantee of ethical behavior. One can know how to behave ethically, know all the virtues, name all the commandments of the various faith traditions, and recite codes of honor, and still behave in corrupt and cruel ways. Moral *ideas* don't necessarily lead to moral *actions*.

Real-life situations have their own demands and create their own moral issues that can't be resolved by the mind alone. The mind can be used to imagine good, to discern the right thing to do, to take the perspective of another, to see the larger picture, to work through complex moral issues, to help to make moral judgments, and to figure out a better way. The role of the mind is then to inform the heart; the mind cannot itself create caring. Reason is called into service by the heart to discern how to act on what the heart knows. The head and heart must work in tandem, with our ability to reason always at the service of our deep caring.

What a person professes and holds true in his mind is not always a strong predictor of how he will act in a given circumstance, or across a wide range of circumstances. Some people have shocked even themselves when they've risen to the occasion and behaved with moral courage at a time when it was most needed and least expected. Sixteen-year-old Simone was known for his quick temper. He was attending an alternative high school after having got into numerous fights at his old school. One day Simone saw a much larger boy pull a gun on the principal, and he wrestled the student to the ground. After it was all over and the other boy was being led away in handcuffs, Simone shook his head and said, "Wow, I can't believe I did it. But I couldn't let him shoot her. No man, that just wouldn't be right." Simone acted with his heart and mind together in the interests of deep caring.

The mind can also be used to construct ways to harm other human beings, to justify bigotry and rationalize prejudice, to validate bias and discrimination. Judging by the vast arsenals of weapons that the human race has amassed and the intricate methods devised by people to torture and dehumanize others, I think we can safely say that knowledge that is not at the service of deep caring is of no service to humanity. Oscar Aris, former president of Costa Rica and winner of the 1987 Nobel peace prize, said, "The siren calls of greed, envy, and sheer power lure us to put our faith in weapons, not ethics; in warfare, not plowshares; in divisions and distrust rather than interdependence and individual responsibility." No matter the information taught, if one does not care to be good, to do good, and to will good, no good will come of such an education.

Two Buddhist monks were walking down a road when they came across a woman who was trying unsuccessfully to cross a swiftly running stream. One monk picked her up, carried her across, and put her down on the other side of the stream. The two monks continued on their way. The second monk grew increasingly agitated. After a short while, the first monk asked the second what was wrong. The second blurted out, "You touched a woman—we took a vow not to touch women." The first monk replied, "Yes, I picked her up, carried her across the stream and put her down. You are still carrying her."

To care deeply is to act not by fixed rules, vows, or laws, but out of deep affection and regard for the weal and the woe of the other. The one monk was concerned with actual human suffering, the other with duty. To anchor one's morality in duty or obligation is to open the possibility of avoiding involvement simply by failing to see a situation as one of duty ("She shouldn't be here all by herself"), by rationalizing or justifying as necessary an action that is mean and cruel ("You're blocking the path—get out of the way so we can get on our way"), or by simply choosing not do a caring act by hiding behind an obligation or duty, as the second monk did ("I took a vow so I can't help her").

HEART

> The heart has its reasons which reason knows
> nothing of.
>
> —BLAISE PASCAL

Nurturing children's ability to care without teaching them to think critically will not serve them well. In his 1963 book *Strength to Love*, Martin Luther King, Jr., wrote, "Nothing in this world is more dangerous than sincere ignorance and conscientious stupidity." Compassion and loving-kindness are emotions that involve both strong feelings and the intellect. Since these are altruistic emotions—for the good of another person—they can rise above other more basic feelings, moods, and thoughts that might affect our inclination to help. Jim was angry that his son carelessly wrecked the car by running it into a post, doing great damage to both. Nevertheless, he cared deeply enough to stand by his son in court. Sue was tired and frustrated as her mom slipped further into Alzheimer's, but her deep caring kept her grounded and kept her being there for her mom every day, and caring enough about herself to get some much needed help and respite care. Even though Mark was frustrated with his younger brother's autistic behavior and embarrassed by his loud outbursts, his deep caring for his brother enabled Mark to be his brother's biggest defender and staunchest ally.

Children can learn to care but without reflection or perspective-taking, be unable to respond effectively to the weal and woe of another. Being conscious of differences but ignorant of commonalities, children might care deeply about those in their tight circle of concern and be fearful of letting in any "outsider."

Without critical thinking skills, moral and ethical dilemmas can leave a child caring deeply and overwhelmed by the magnitude or gravity of a given situation. A child can become depressed and/or apathetic if reason shows him no way to work through the dilemma or to respond.

If a child makes generalizations based on emotional prejudices, rather than observable facts or intelligent inquiry, he is likely to notice in other children only what accords with his prejudices and be blind to everything else. This creates stereotypical expectations, which in turn invite overt discrimination. Such emotional prejudices and stereotypical expectations are extremely resistant to change, even when they come up against concrete evidence or contrary facts.

MESSY EMOTIONS AND INSTINCTS

There are no negative emotions; there are only negative attitudes toward emotions we don't like and can't tolerate, and the negative consequences of denying them. The emotions we call "negative" are energies that get our attention, ask for expression, transmit information and impel action. Grief tells us that we are all interconnected in the web of life, and what connects us also breaks our hearts. Fear alerts us to protect and sustain life. Despair asks us to grieve our losses, to examine and transform the meaning of our lives, to repair our broken souls. Each of these emotions is purposeful and useful—if we know how to listen to them.

—MIRIAM GREENSPAN, "THE WISDOM OF DARK
EMOTIONS," *SHAMBHALA SUN*

Feelings are not "good" or "bad"—they are real. They are vital to our ability to connect with one another and to relate effectively (and affectively) with the world. Children who can express their emotions in a healthy way are more likely to reach out to others and to care, share, help, and comfort more readily than their peers who stifle their emotions or who are explosive and unpredictable. It matters what children are taught to do with all of their feelings.

When parents demand obedience and rule by fear, children are taught at a young age not to express their true feelings. Spontaneous expressions of joy, concern, and happiness are stifled, because all feelings are stifled. Anger hostility, opposition, and sadness are all punished. Eventually the child becomes so wary of her parents that *no* feelings are spontaneously expressed; she must first check in to see if the feeling is okay.

If forbidden to express emotions, kids get stuck in their anger, fear, sadness, and hurt. Sometimes they even refuse to acknowledge that they are angry or hurt and have no way of getting rid of the energy produced by those feelings. The energy builds up inside like steam pressure in a boiler. Eventually one of three things will happen:

1. Passive-destructive acts against the self. Instead of solving the problem, passive-destructive acts destroy the person who has the problem. (Self-mutilation; depression; somatic illness; personal put-downs: "I'm no good," "I'm stupid.")
2. Aggressive acts against others deliberately intended to harm. Aggressive acts don't solve the original

problem and they tend to create new ones. (Fighting, hitting, biting.)
3. Passive-aggressive acts. These acts combine the passive-destructive and aggressive in a way that signals that the person is responsible neither for himself nor for others. The passive-aggressive individual destroys herself physically, mentally, and emotionally; harms others; and creates more problems. (Violating a confidence and spreading a rumor in order to harm the other person, but saying, "I didn't mean to hurt you. You're being too sensitive about it.")

Some parents express their own feelings and respond to their child's feelings in an extreme way by smothering the child or owning his feelings for him. This parent will not encourage her child to work through his own feelings ("Don't be sad, I'll get you another pet"), or she will protect him from the consequences of the expression of those feelings ("It's his own fault that you hit him. I'll talk with the principal and I won't let them suspend you"). Sometimes the parent's feelings and the child's feelings get intertwined. The child gets confused about whose feelings are whose. Trying to keep a parent happy, a child becomes overly aware of others' feelings at the expense of his own self-awareness. He learns that his own feelings are not as important as other people's. He learns to take care of others at the expense of his own mental and physical well-being.

If a parent constantly rescues a child from feelings and situations, the child learns to be dependent on others to define her own feelings. She becomes helpless at solving her own problems and quick to lay blame on others. Eventually the child begins to feel angry and resentful at not being truly listened to; she begins to doubt her own feelings and either leaves it up to others to pick up the pieces, or attacks those who suggest that she is capable of handling her own problems.

If a parent abandons or neglects the child, the child learns to put aside or hide feelings of fear, hurt, sorrow, and anger, because they get in the way of taking care of the parent's feelings and thus being able to stay connected. He learns not to trust others and to manipulate them to get what he needs. Joy, concern, and happiness are smothered. The child becomes either too self-sufficient, allowing no intimacy into his life, or an extremely needy person, constantly seeking others to make him feel safe, loved, and secure. He goes through the motions of living but neglects his mind and body, or becomes a bully, or at worst, he becomes a hollow shell of a human being without remorse and with terrible vengeance, who strikes out at anyone and anything in his way.

Nurturing parents regularly do five things:

1. They acknowledge their own feelings and label them ("I'm angry," "I'm hurt," "I'm upset," "I'm happy," "I'm sad," "I'm frustrated," "I'm worried"). They express a full range of emotions. Children see them laughing, crying, joyful, sad, angry, hurt, frustrated. Kids learn it is all right to feel and express their feelings.

2. They can admit that they are angry, or hurt, or afraid, and then do something responsible and purposeful to address those feelings. In this way, kids learn that there are constructive ways to work through feelings. They don't need to deny or make excuses for their own feelings.

3. They make assertive statements about themselves ("I can do this," "I can handle it," "I blew it this time, and I'll fix it," "I can accept it"). These statements create a sense of power and help children to master— not control—their feelings.

4. They acknowledge that their children's feelings are real and legitimate without passing judgment on those feelings ("You seem to be really sad about your friend moving away. Would you like to sit here and be held, or would you rather be alone for a while?"). Kids learn that their own feelings are important, that they can be trusted to handle those feelings, and that it is okay to count on others for support.

5. They teach their children to handle their own feelings assertively. When kids express their feelings irresponsibly, nurturing parents accept those feelings as real, label the feelings, and help their children find alternative expressions that are both responsible and assertive. Sometimes helping kids arrive at alternative actions means starting at the beginning with simply identifying a feeling and affirming a child's right to that feeling ("You seem really angry," "It's okay to cry when you feel sad," "I know it is frustrating to have to leave your friend's house when you are having so much fun").

Kids who know that their own feelings are important are more likely to respect other children's feelings. They are also more likely to resonate with *(empathize)* or respond to *(sympathize)* their peers, and thus are more likely to show compassion and loving-kindness than their peers who have learned to suppress, intellectualize, judge, or deny their own feelings.

Instincts play a large part in helping us "read" the environment around us, including other people's feelings. Paul Ekman, a professor emeritus of psychology at the University of California in San Francisco, discovered that facial expressions for seven emotions—anger, fear, sadness, disgust, surprise, contempt, and happiness—are the same around the world. Mimicry is the biological mechanism that causes us from infancy, and throughout our lives, to imitate the facial expressions, postures, and voices of the people around us. In their book *Emotional Contagion*, authors Elaine Hatfield, John T. Cacioppo, and Richard L. Rapson wrote, "People susceptible to others' yawns are more likely to be empathetic." That is, they seem particularly vulnerable to "catching emotion." Others are better at emitting emotions. And negative emotions are usually more "infectious" than positive ones, thus the emphasis in literature on empathic distress in infants as the root of empathy. But actually, it is our instinct to mimic (or catch) all types of emotions that provides the foundation for us to be able to resonate with and to understand someone else's feelings.

For our ancestors, the *fright, flight, or fight* mechanism helped to keep them alive and reproducing. Today these instincts can serve us well if we allow them to tune us in to immediate danger. Seeing what looks to be a rattlesnake on the trail, without thought, our bodies go into a healthy fear mode. We don't wait to think about whether it is a rope, a garter snake, or a deadly rattler—we move, then look more closely, and either relax at the sight of the rope or keep moving in the opposite direction. It is when we become full of fright, or we keep fleeing from some pervasive threat—imaginary or not—that we are no longer able to care deeply or share generously or help willingly. When we allow our fear to capture our imagination, our thinking, and our feelings, we are more likely to get caught up in the hating, hoarding, and harming—the three virulent agents that can rip apart the fabric of human relationships.

> The place to improve the world is first in one's own heart and head and hands.
> —ROBERT M. PERSIG, *ZEN AND THE ART OF MOTORCYCLE MAINTENANCE*

Chapter 2

Being Good, Doing Good

THE BIG I AND THE THREE CS

[I]f we are unable to connect with others to some
extent, if we cannot at least imagine the potential
impact of our actions on others, then we have no
means to discriminate between right and wrong,
between what is appropriate and what is not,
between harming and non-harming.
—HIS HOLINESS THE DALAI LAMA,
ETHICS FOR THE NEW MILLENNIUM

An act that harms or does violence to other human beings,
causing or increasing their suffering or depriving them of
joy, is potentially an unethical act.

Melissa and Anita made up a game only two could play.
They didn't want Jesse to play with them because Jesse played
with the new girl yesterday. Melissa and Anita could say that
there was nothing wrong with making up a game only two
can play. And they would be right. It's not wrong to make up
a game only two can play. But it's not right if Melissa and
Anita's *intent* was to purposely exclude another child.

Intent matters. It is what drives and inspires our actions.
Most of the time, intent is the most important of the four

elements that come into play when determining the ethical nature of an act. The other three—content, circumstance, and consequence—are subordinate to intent.

The **content** of an activity contributes to the degree that the act either harms or does violence to deep caring (shunning Jesse, turning their backs on her, telling her in a rude way that she couldn't join them, lying to her, or simply announcing that only two could play their game). The **circumstance** can mitigate the act (*where* the act took place—on a crowded playground, at Jesse's home, in Melissa's yard; *when* it took place—immediately after the girls had excluded Jesse from the lunch table, a day after Jesse had excluded Anita from a game, the morning the teacher and the bus driver had reprimanded Jesse).

In most cases, **consequences**, both intended and unintended, are the least relevant factors in determining the ethical nature of the act. Rarely can the fruits of our actions be attributed solely to the person(s) doing the deed (Jesse cried and felt isolated; the new girl invited Jesse to join a different group to play an exciting game; the teacher caught the girls in their mean act; in anger and hurt, Jesse kicked dirt into the eyes of the two girls; Jesse, having Asperger's syndrome, was oblivious to social cues and was unaware that she had been shunned; or she recognized Melissa's and Anita's meanness and decided it was their problem, not hers). It is important to note that just because a child is unaware that the girls have been mean and cruel to her doesn't make their intent any less unethical, nor does it change the unethical nature of their act.

Changing the intent *does* change the ethical nature of an act. If Melissa and Anita are playing a game, unaware that they are leaving Jesse out, that unawareness is not *intended* to harm. It's what they do if Jesse asks to join that will show their "ethical colors." If Jesse asks to be included, the girls could welcome her to join or kindly tell her that their game can only be played by two people. She is welcome to watch, and she can play with one of them at the next recess. They could also sneer at her, turn their backs, and pretend not to hear, or make an unkind remark directed at her.

Engrossed in play is one thing. Being so self-centered that the concerns of others are not on their list of things to be aware of is quite another. This self-centeredness can contribute to the girls' inability to see the suffering *(empathy)* of another child or to feel badly that the girl is hurting *(sympathy)*, or to feel any need to help alleviate her pain *(compassion)*—or to prevent the suffering in the first place *(loving-kindness)*.

This unawareness might cause little if any harm if the girls are young, not very socially adept, and still trying to figure out the rituals and manners of play. Nevertheless, you can't ignore such lack of awareness lest the girls begin to develop the habit of tuning others out and becoming engrossed only in matters that concern them directly. The harm might be huge if this unawareness is obliviousness due to a narrow-minded bigotry that renders Jesse invisible to them. Narrow-minded bigotry that renders another human invisible is one of the hallmarks of hate.

The content of the act might weigh heavily when determining the ethical nature of that act. If Melissa and Anita are home alone after school and decide to make up a game only two can play so that they won't be bored, their intent is good and so is the circumstance. If they decide that the game is to spread ugly rumors in a chat room on the Internet, then the content is mean and cruel, and the consequences might be destructive, not only to the girl they "flame" but also to their own ethical selves. Their intent to find something to do to ease their boredom was good; what they did (content) created an opportunity for a new intent, different circumstances, and more consequences to be reckoned with.

The intent and content might be wholesome and good, but the circumstances might raise a red flag. If the two girls decide to make up a fun game that only the two of them can play, there is nothing wrong with the intent or the content. But if they are playing this game in the middle of the class field trip as the museum guide is explaining the latest dinosaur exhibit, it is not right. The dynamic changes again if the game they are playing is intended and designed to help them remember what they saw on the tour.

Consequences are often the least important factor in determining the ethical nature of an act, simply because consequences are not solely dependent on the actions of the person performing the deed. Intended and unintended consequences are often the result of the interactions between all of the people involved, occasionally with bystanders, and certainly with the social and cultural environment. If the girls created a game that only two could play and they gently explained to Jesse that she could play the game with one of them at the next recess, there is no guarantee that Jesse won't go and tell the teacher that the girls were not being fair. Their intent, content, and circumstance were all good. The outcome for the two girls might have nothing to do with the fact that their actions were honorable. What they can cling to, even in the face of Jesse's accusation, is that their behavior was ethical.

The abstract absolute right or absolute wrong ("Always tell the truth," "Don't ever lie") is so much easier and more efficient than dealing with the concrete here and now. But it is in the concrete that ethical thinking and acting take place. And if that thinking and acting is rooted in deep caring, chances are the actions will be ethical.

Teaching children how to utilize the Big I and the Three Cs won't tell them what to think or how to act. In the same way, knowing an algebraic formula won't give children the answer to a math problem, only a way to find an answer to any number of math problems. Knowing how to utilize the Big I and the Three Cs will give them a way to discern an answer and possible actions. The two girls and their game is a simple example. Giving young children opportunities to practice with such everyday ethical situations will help them tackle the bigger issues (friendships, sexual relationships, standing up for another child or against an injustice); more complex situations, where there are competing needs or more than one "Thou" in the mix (deciding whether to help Grandma or babysit for the neighbor who is ill); moral temptations and dilemmas (cheating or not cheating is a temptation; when two or more virtues clash it's a dilemma). Your children will also discover that just because something is *not wrong* doesn't necessarily make it *right*; just because they *can* do something doesn't mean they *should*; just because they have *a right* to do something doesn't make it the *right thing* to do; and there is never a *right way* to do the *wrong thing*.

Just because you have the right to do something or say
something, does not make it the right thing to do....
[L]aw is an ethical consensus in a community, which is
then articulated and enforced ... it reflects what is
prohibited and what is not.... [E]thics reflects a higher
standard than the law.
—U.S. SUPREME COURT JUSTICE POTTER STEWART

TO ACT OR NOT TO ACT

The idea that people decide to adopt their moral
principles seems to me to be a myth, a psychological
shadow thrown by a logical distinction; and if
someone did claim to have done this, I think I would
be justified in doubting either the truth of what he
said or the reality of those moral principles. We see a
man's genuine convictions as coming from somewhere
deeper in him than that.
—BERNARD WILLIAMS, "MORALITY AND
EMOTIONS," IN *PROBLEMS OF THE SELF*

It is difficult to discern if an action is a right action or a
harmful one if we don't take into consideration the potential consequences as well as our intent, the content of our
actions, and the circumstances—*before* we act. Although
we can't know or control all of the possible intended or
unintended consequences in the short term or long term,
we do know that if our actions have the potential to hurt
another person, or if our actions have the potential to
relieve their suffering, those actions will make a difference
in both of our lives.

If we conclude that our actions could harm another person and we commence to act, we come full circle to our intent to harm. We have not only harmed the other, we have violated our own sense of self as one who cares. If we conclude that our actions could help relieve the suffering of the other, we have three choices: to not act; to act because we want to maintain our *image* as a caring person; or to act to help relieve the suffering of the other, because we *must*.

1. TO NOT ACT

It is not only for what we do that we are held responsible, but also for what we don't do.

—MOLIÈRE

To not act is in reality an act of *allowing suffering* to continue unabated when we could help. A 1995 Toronto, Ontario, study on bullying found that only 13 percent of peers intervened in an episode of bullying at which they were present. The question that begs to be asked is: Why would 87 percent of the kids who would not instigate bullying be so willing to become a part of the attack or turn a blind eye to the plight of the targeted child?

There are a few valid reasons and lots of excuses. The four reasons most often given for not intervening:

1. The bystander is afraid of getting hurt.
2. The bystander is afraid of becoming a new target of the bully.

3. The bystander is afraid of doing something that will only make the situation worse.
4. The bystander does not know what to do.

As legitimate as they are, these reasons do not shore up the self-confidence or self-respect that is eroded when a child witnesses harm done to a peer and is unable or unwilling to respond effectively to stop the cruelty. All too often these fears and lack of skill can turn into apathy—a potent friend of contempt. Contempt grows best in a climate of indifference.

Bystanders have more excuses than valid reasons for not intervening. These excuses help poison the social environment, increasing the likelihood that bystanders will side with the bully and eventually assume the role of bullies themselves. They include but are certainly not limited to these nine:

1. *The bully is a friend*. Kids are less willing to intervene when the bully is seen as a friend, even if this friend is being unfair or disrespectful.
2. *It's not my problem. This is not my fight*. Socialized not to interfere in other people's affairs, to do their own work, and to look out for number one, bystanders can excuse themselves by claiming to mind their own business. This is also known as indifference.
3. *She is not my friend*. Kids are more willing to intervene when the targeted kid is a friend. Bullies often target kids who have few friends.
4. *He's a loser*. In a highly competitive culture it is easy to write off targets as "losers." Bystanders fear they might

lose their own status in their group if they are even seen with the targeted child, let alone seen defending her.

5. *She deserved to be bullied, asked for it, had it coming.* Why stop when something is warranted? She didn't even stand up for herself, so why would anyone else stand up for her? This excuse appears to get the bystander off the hook, but it fails to take into account the basic principle that bullying is about contempt. No one deserves to be stripped of her dignity and self-worth. Targeted kids cannot always act alone to successfully fend off a bully or bullies.

6. *Bullying will toughen him up.* Bullying does not toughen up a target; it humiliates and often enrages him. The target might become what is known as "the bullied bully" and not strike back in anger but with cold, calculating contempt.

7. *Who wants to be called a snitch or a rat?* Kids have a deeply embedded code of silence and often won't risk being blamed for getting someone else in trouble. What isn't considered in this excuse is the immorality of silence in the face of malice.

8. *It's better to be in the in-group than to defend the outcasts.* In a clique, once the leader of the pack identifies a kid as a target, the rest of the group tends to fall mindlessly in line, doing the bully's bidding without much consideration for the rights and feelings of the outcast. The in-group becomes so tightly connected and single-minded that there is no room for protest, dissent, or differences. The need for approval and acceptance within such a clique is so strong that even if the bystander felt the momentary urge to protest the

harm being done to a targeted kid, that urge would be quickly squelched. When cliques are the norm, there is a clear demarcation of "us," "them," and "kids below us and them," who are thus deserving of contempt and certainly not worthy of concern.

9. *It's too big a pain in the brain.* A bystander must weigh the pros and cons of remaining faithful to the group versus siding with the targeted kid. This mental calculation can create tremendous emotional tension. The fastest way to reduce the tension is to magnify the pros of marching lockstep with the group and magnify the cons of helping out the bullied kid.

Add the four legitimate reasons to the first eight excuses and the answer seems simple—don't get involved. Added bonus—the headache is gone. In her prologue to *Rescuers: Portraits of Moral Courage in the Holocaust*, Cynthia Ozick writes of the dangers of allowing such suffering: "Indifference finally grows lethal ... the act of turning away, however empty-handed and harmlessly, remains nevertheless an act."

2. TO ACT TO MAINTAIN OUR *IMAGE* AS A CARING PERSON

It doesn't take long for children to discover that appearing or seeming to appear appropriate brings as much approval and avoids as much disapproval as actually *being* appropriate. Perhaps that is the birth of hypocrisy ...

—A. LYNN SCORESBY, *BRINGING UP MORAL CHILDREN IN AN IMMORAL WORLD*

When threats and bribes are used in an attempt to control behavior, children not only learn ways to avoid getting caught doing something wrong, they figure out ways to get caught doing something good so that they can get praise, recognition, and tangible rewards for their "good deeds." It's all about getting caught—learning to work the system for the payoff—not about being kind or helpful. Caring acts become means to an end—ways to make a child "look good." If there is no payoff, there is little if any inclination to act.

Research has repeatedly shown that children who are rewarded for acts of generosity will be less likely to think of themselves as caring people and more likely to be less generous when there are no rewards to be had. Extrinsic rewards tend to decrease intrinsic motivation, including the motivation to care. The concern is not for the person in need, but how caring for that person makes the "caring" person look. In a recent article in the *New York Times*, twelfth-graders were describing the various community service activities they were involved in during their high school years. Many of them said that one of the main incentives for doing these activities was to "look good" on their college applications or to "compete on a level playing field with other 'do-gooders'" applying for the coveted spots at prestigious universities.

In his book *Education*, Immanuel Kant wrote about the dangers of rewarding a child for being good: "[H]e will do right merely for the sake of the reward; and when he goes out into the world and finds that goodness is not always rewarded, nor wickedness always punished, he will grow into a man who only thinks about how he may get on in the world, and does right or wrong according as he finds advantage to himself." Finding advantage to oneself is not deep caring—even of oneself. C. Daniel Batson and his colleagues concluded in their study *Buying Kindness: Effects of an Extrinsic Incentive for Helping on Perceived Altruism*: "A person's kindness, it seems, cannot be bought." And the *image* of oneself as a caring person is a cheap substitute for the real thing.

3. TO ACT FOR THE BENEFIT OF THE OTHER PERSON

You cannot do a kindness too soon because you never know how soon it will be too late.
                                                    —RALPH WALDO EMERSON

When we act for the benefit of others, our intention is other-regarding rather than self-centered: "Because she lives alone and has no grandkids to visit her." "Because he was hungry." "Because he needed help." It does not mean that we won't benefit from the action—we might or might not; in most cases, we probably will—but the *intention* is for the good of the other.

Speaking and doing what is right when the burden is heavy is never easy at any age. Doing what is decent, caring, and compassionate *in spite of* external consequences and never merely *because of them* requires openness to the person who is suffering, and a willingness to respond with the concern, the care, and the help that that person needs.

Six-year-old Peter grabbed the pacifier out of six-month-old Michael's mouth. Peter stood back laughing at the crying baby. Almost-four-year-old Rebecca stomped over to Peter, grabbed the pacifier, and said, "You're mean." She then put the pacifier in Michael's mouth and tried to soothe him. Rebecca wasn't old enough to rationally assess the risk she might be taking in seizing the pacifier from Peter. To her, a baby was in distress and she knew she could do something to help relieve that distress. As young as she was, her action was a *must* for her.

Refusing to stand idly by or to join in, eight-year-old Josh told Billy that he wasn't going along with the plan to deliberately exclude the new boy from their recess basketball game. "It's mean to do that to him. We can all play." Billy then told Josh he would have to pick between playing with that "sissy" or with the rest of the boys. Josh stood his ground and insisted that they all play together. After lashing out at Josh and getting nowhere, the bully backed down.

Fifteen-year-old Beth watched in horror as her friends picked up their trays en masse and moved to another table, jeering at the unpopular girl who had dared to sit down at "their" table. Seeing the hurt in the ostracized girl's eyes, Beth remained at the table and talked with her as her peers rolled their eyes in disgust at such traitorous behavior.

Both Beth and Josh were willing to stand up, step in, and speak out, knowing that if they took a stand, others might follow. They also recognized that even if no one else followed in their footsteps, they would still do whatever was necessary to ease the suffering and pain of their classmates who were targeted. Their empathy, sympathy, and compassion involved taking a stand and taking action. Both kids were willing to do something to alleviate the pain they saw, even at the expense of alienating friends. They chose doing good over looking good in the eyes of their peers.

In an interview for an article in *Newsweek* magazine three years after the shootings at Columbine High School in Littleton, Colorado, writer Susannah Meadows spoke with several students whose older siblings had survived the shootings. They appeared to be far more vigilant than their peers when it came to stopping bullying and other acts of meanness or cruelty at their school. She wrote about Ty Werges, a sophomore on the soccer team, and how he came upon some kids slamming shut the locker of a student who was mentally impaired. "I was like, 'Why are you doing that? Do you feel cool now?' They were shocked because out of nowhere someone sticking up for another kid is kind of weird. But the bullying stopped." Choosing to be a witness—with all the risks that could entail—instead of a bystander, Ty Werges was able to help alleviate the pain of a classmate—and perhaps cool some of that targeted teenager's rage.

During the summer of 2004, after three hurricanes had hit a small town in Florida and another was on its way, plywood prices skyrocketed, leaving many people on limited incomes unable to afford the wood to board up their windows. The owner of a small lumber company opened up his yard and gave away the plywood. He told people to take only what they needed, but take all that they needed. TV commentators speculated that the man had to be doing this for some self-serving reason. Was it to get media attention? To encourage repeat business after the hurricane? When pressed by a reporter to give a reason, the owner said he didn't have time to talk—he was too busy giving away wood. The reporter asked one of the teenage sales clerks why he thought the owner was being so generous—what was his motive? The clerk merely shrugged his shoulders and replied, "Because he has a big heart." Unsatisfied with that explanation, the reporter once again pressed the owner for an answer. The man said simply, "Because they need the wood." For the owner there was no cost-benefit analysis, no eye to a tax write-off, no ulterior motive, no *should* or *ought* to make him give his wood away. For him it became a *must*—a compelling need to ease the suffering of other human beings in his community.

When one is helpless to do anything medically for someone who is dying, simply being present to them in their suffering—caring for their physical needs, listening to their story, and helping them to find some comfort and peace in their final passage through life—might be the most deeply caring act possible at the time. When Peg told her younger brother Cliff that she was dying of breast cancer that had spread to her brain, Cliff recoiled at the thought of seeing her in such a painful state and decided he would rather "remember her in death as she was when she was healthy." No stark memories of seeing his sister emaciated and in horrific pain for him. He called her regularly and sent her small gifts. One day his mother called and said that his sister was asking for him, and only him. Steeling himself, he flew out to be with her for her final weeks. He spent the time caring for her, giving her pain medicine, laughing with her, crying with her, and finally holding her as she died. The deep caring was a gift to the both of them.

Fourteen-year-old Ali saw a young boy fall into a swollen mountain stream and be thrown against a huge rock. Jumping into the raging waters, she grabbed the little boy and held onto him until a rescue team pulled them both out. The young boy died later that day. Trying to save another person's life, doing everything humanly possible but failing, left the young girl devastated. Onlookers judged her actions to be either stupid, crazy, irresponsible, or heroic. It mattered not to the failed rescuer. It was the jumping into the stream in an attempt to save the little boy that was important. For her, to have stood by and watched would have been unfathomable.

COMMON DECENCY IN THE NOW

> When will our consciences grow so tender that we
> will act to prevent misery rather than avenge it?
> —ELEANOR ROOSEVELT

In *The Plague*, one of Albert Camus's characters, Dr. Rieux, is asked why he is willing to risk his own life to care for plague victims. He replies: "I have no idea what's awaiting me, or what will happen when this all ends. For the moment, I know this: There are sick people and they need curing…. There's no question of heroism in all this. It is a matter of common decency … [which] consists in doing my job…. Heroism and sanctity don't really appeal to me, I imagine. What interests me is being a man."

A matter of common decency in the moment is what an ethic rooted in deep caring is about: the I and Thou, the We in the now. One of Russia's greatest novelists and one of its most influential moral philosophers and social reformers, Leo Tolstoy, writes of this common decency in the moment is his short story "The Three Questions." A king is looking for the answer to life's most pressing questions: "It once occurred to a certain king, that if he knew the right time to begin everything; if he knew who were the right people to listen to, and whom to avoid; and above all, if he always knew what was the most important thing to do, he would never fail in anything he might undertake." After asking learned men, who all answer his questions differently, the king heads into the forest to ask a hermit.

During his time in the forest, the king unwittingly rescues someone who is trying to harm him. By saving his enemy, he creates a profound connection with this man. Not knowing he has found the answers to his questions, the king returns to the hermit and asks him once again. The hermit replies: "Do you not see?... [T]here is only one time that is important—Now! It is the most important time because it is the only time when we have any power. The most necessary man is he with whom you are, for no man knows whether he will ever have dealings with any one else: and the most important affair is, to do him good, because for that purpose alone was man sent into this life."

> There may be a time off from the call of duty, but no time off from the demand of good. The capacity to seek and enjoy the good and the true is versatile and endlessly creative.
>
> —IRIS MURDOCH

WOW AND WHY

The fairest thing we can experience is the mysterious. It is the fundamental emotion, which stands at the

cradle of true art and true science. He who knows it not
and can no longer wonder, no longer feel amazement,
is as good as dead, a snuffed-out candle.
                        —ALBERT EINSTEIN, *IDEAS AND OPINIONS*

It might be heartening for parents, who often feel that they
spend large amounts of time issuing directives and making
rules, to learn that the realm of ethical thinking is not the
exclusive domain of adults, but is in fact a natural place for
children. A sense of wonder and healthy skepticism are part
and parcel of a child's developing sense of fairness and
justice, and need not be lost as a child grows. It is natural for
children to ask why, to seek the ethical reasons upon which
to build their lives, to find out what really matters and why
it matters.

Commenting about children's need to have a sense of
purpose and direction in life, a set of values grounded in
moral introspection, Dr. Robert Coles writes in *The Moral
Intelligence of Children*, "In fact, moral exploration, not to
mention wonder about this life's various mysteries, its
ironies and ambiguities, its complexities and paradoxes—
such activity of the mind and heart make for the experience
of what a human being is: the creature of awareness who,
through language, or distinctive capabilities, probes for
patterns and themes, for the significance of things."

One of the amazing things about three-year-olds is their
ever-present sense of wonder and skepticism—that *wow* and
why of life. "Wow, look at the worm." "Wow, look at the
sky." "Wow, look at the mess." "Why is she sad?" "Why did
he go?" "Why can't I?" These wows and whys are necessary
to help children develop their own sense of purpose and

direction in life. Keeping these gifts of wonder and skepticism alive in our children is essential to their well-being.

During the elementary years, children can keep their sense of wonder alive by exploring nature and studying the solar system, by becoming involved in the arts, by reading fantasy and adventure stories, and creating their own plays with their own costumes, music, programs, and stage settings. It is during these years that children are fascinated by the human body and the wonder of how it is put together and how it works. The more they are amazed by their own bodies and the human family, with its differences and similarities, the wonders of the planet they live on and the neighborhoods they explore, the more likely they are to respect, not harm, any of it. The more they are invited to question, to think critically and independently as well as work collaboratively, the more likely they are to see themselves as responsible, resourceful, resilient human beings capable of being good and doing good.

RATIONALIZING VS. REASONING

A teenager who has a sense of wonder about life is less likely to harm himself and others. With his skepticism intact, when friends ask him to vandalize the school building, he is more likely to ask, "Why would I do that?" With that, his critical thinking skills become engaged. These skills in turn help him to discern the good, the right, and the just thing to do in the face of such peer pressure. If his critical thinking skills are at the service of his deep caring, he will not be merely weighing the odds of getting caught, or wondering how to avoid being mocked by his peers for being "chicken."

It is easy—and tempting—for a teen to rationalize and justify his way out of making a diffcult ethical choice ("I'll go along and just watch, that way I won't have any paint on me if we get caught," "Everybody does this kind of stuff sometime in their teen years," "It's only an old building—no harm done," "If I don't go along, I'll never live it down").

Rationalizing is not the same as **reasoning**. A rationalized decision will be logical and internally consistent, but it might be divorced entirely from the bigger picture. It is taking into account the complicated context in which we make our decisions—our intentions in doing something, the consequences that might follow, the effect on our relationships with others—that makes them reasonable.

But if a teen's thinking skills are at the service of deep caring, they are not so readily available for rationalizing. His thoughts are more likely to be reasonable, his actions difficult and ethical.

"WHY CAN'T I?"

> Once you have learned how to ask questions—relevant and appropriate and substantial questions—you have learned how to learn, and no one can keep you from learning whatever you want or need to know.
> —NEIL POSTMAN AND CHARLES WEINGARTNER,
> *TEACHING AS A SUBVERSIVE ACTIVITY*

One of the most valuable questions that kids ask as they navigate through the wows and whys is "Why can't I?" It's a question that opens the door to parents and children sharing their thoughts, ideas, and feelings and exploring some ideas about right and wrong together. But when the answer is

"Because I said so," that door slams shut. "Because I said so" is a lousy answer that teaches children nothing about taking advantage of their healthy skepticism. It also reinforces the notion that a child's answers to ethical choices lie outside of herself, that those answers need not make any sense, and that they do not necessarily give any direction for what is a good way to behave. Lynn Leight, the author of *Raising Sexually Healthy Children*, puts the issue of ethical choices in the framework of four answers to that question: *Why can't I?*

1. Because it is unkind. (The two girls shun their class-mate on the playground.)
2. Because it is hurtful. (The eight-year-old trips his younger sister as she races to the car.)
3. Because it is unfair. (The twelve-year-old cuts his piece of the pie bigger than his two siblings' pieces.)
4. Because it is dishonest. (A teenager downloads his science project off the Internet and submits it as his own.)

Each one of these answers gives children a tool to help keep both their thinking and their actions rooted in their own deep caring. The answers are not a set of rules or laws. In *Ethics for the New Millennium*, His Holiness the Dalai Lama writes of the infinite complexity of reality. Function-ing from a formulaic approach—devising a set of rules or laws in an attempt to provide us with answers to every ethical choice or dilemma—does not allow us to "capture the richness and diversity of the human experience." It is impossible to make enough rules to cover all of the tempta-tions, and not all questions have answers. An ethic rooted in deep caring takes us far beyond the rules and beyond mere adherence to laws. We are challenged to see things less in terms of right and wrong and more in terms of a complex interlinking of relationships and guidelines.

Each one of the examples given above—shunning, tripping, hoarding, and cheating—present a "teachable moment." The nurturing parent can help his children work through repairing the damage they have done by each of these acts, the harm they have caused, or the pain they have inflicted— in essence, to own it and fix it, and then to learn from it. The learning is often the hard part, for both the parent and the child. In a conversation with Robert Coles, author and psychoanalyst Eric Erickson described the difficulty this way: "It's a long haul, bringing up our children to be good; you have to keep doing that, *bring them up*, and that means *bringing things up with them*."

"Bringing things up" will include not only what your children have done to cause harm to themselves or to others, but also how they can show kindness, compassion, fairness, and honesty or trustworthiness. As children are invited to demonstrate these behaviors in a greater variety of ways, and as they increasingly witness siblings, peers, and adults playing them out, they will build a larger repertoire of caring experiences. These will be memories that they can ground themselves in as they learn to see themselves as cared for and capable of loving-kindness and compassion. With these experiences firmly in place, when kids are confronted with important questions and problems for which answers and solutions are not readily available, they are more likely to exercise their critical thinking skills and less likely to succumb to us/them, good/bad, right/wrong stereotypes and prejudices. And they are less inclined to accept "Because I said so" as a valid answer.

There are questions that have no discernable answers in the present. Sometimes it is a matter of taking time to be silent, to reflect, and just be willing to be present and not act. In stillness we can sometimes be more aware of a bigger picture. Sometimes possibilities that didn't present themselves in the midst of a major problem come forward during the still moments. And sometimes possibilities that didn't exist at the moment of a crisis come together to create an even better resolution than was possible when the crisis first loomed large. In stillness, kids can learn to be open to those possibilities.

Turning around the question of "Why can't I?" in his book *Can We Be Good Without God?*, Canadian physician Dr. Robert Buckman asks the question "Why should I behave decently?" His answer: "Because it will be a better world for the human race if we all do."

It is with each other's protection that people live.
—JOHN DOYLE, *THE GLOBE AND MAIL*

AGES AND STAGES

The past is a foreign country. They do things differently there.
—L. P. HARTLEY, PROLOGUE TO *THE GO-BETWEEN*

Through children's early interactions and dialogues with their parents, caregivers, and peers they learn how to care deeply, share generously, and help willingly. During the various ages and stages of childhood, children develop their own moral sensibilities and concerns about fairness, honesty, kindness, and injustice. Their emotional responses, and those they evoke in others by their behavior, help them to develop a range of emotions that facilitate rather than hinder thinking and acting ethically.

INFANTS

Morality is not something that can be imposed on children. Instead, it is nurtured and grown from within human social relationships. The first relationship we experience is between mother and child. When a mother takes care of herself and creates a home that is welcoming before her child is born, she signals to her infant that he or she is cared for deeply. The infant takes it from there.

It is in us to care. Babies only a few days old respond to another baby who is not just cranky but truly in distress. Infants appear to have the inborn capacity to vicariously experience the feelings of others. Since they lack the clear distinction between themselves and the person who is in distress, they respond as though they themselves were in distress. Instead of one baby crying, you now have two. In his book *Empathy and Moral Development: Implications for Caring and Justice*, Martin L. Hoffman describes this empathic distress, or "reactive cry," and refers to it as "the spark of human concern for others, the glue that makes social life possible. It may be fragile but it has, arguably, endured throughout evolutionary times." This spark of human concern is also lit when infants as young as four months old see a human face that shows sadness or distress. They often look away, which is a classic baby sign of distress.

It is this spark of human concern that needs to be nurtured in order for children to develop empathy, sympathy, compassion, and healthy guilt—which in turn become the emotional underpinnings for prosocial behavior. The repetitive pairing of a child's empathic distress with another's distress helps children develop an "expectation of distress" when they see another suffering in grief or pain. If this spark is kept alive, it contributes an almost instinctual, involuntary dimension to a child's responses later on when he or she sees someone in distress. This is in part why we cry at the movies, even when we've "set our mind" not to cry. And this should give us pause when we hear ourselves telling our sons, "Big boys don't cry," or "Stop crying or I'll give you something to cry about."

Yes, this spark can be beaten out of a child, or covered over with a lot of muck (bigotry, prejudice, and hatred), to the point that the child no longer has the expectation of distress when she sees someone in distress, or no feelings of guilt when she causes someone pain. When this spark is doused, instead of distress, what you might see is a child getting pleasure from another's pain, inflicting the pain to get that pleasure, or having an apathetic response to another's pain.

We see signs of empathic distress still in operation in adults when we are on an airplane that is descending to land. As a baby cries in pain, most of us on the plane are visibly distressed—many of us are feeling badly for both the baby and the parent; others are wishing we could soothe the baby ourselves; some offer advice about giving the baby something to suck on; some give a sympathetic smile to the mom to let her know we have been there too; and some display their own distress in an obnoxious manner ("Give me a stiff drink. I don't know why they let babies fly on planes. I can't stand that crying"). The obnoxious ones are still showing signs of distress—it's just that the distress is all about themselves being bothered, not about caring for the one who is in real distress.

The loving-kindness a parent demonstrates by nurturing the infant and responding compassionately to the infant's distress helps newborns begin to construct the patterns of moral internalization that will enable them to develop, in the months and years to come, the ability to more fully care for and about others, to feel responsible (able to respond) and connected to others. The way adults respond to a baby's distress with soothing words and actions begins to teach her how to respond to someone else's distress. The way adults express loving-kindness teaches her that she is lovable and gives her ways to express her own loving-kindness toward others.

Between nine and twelve months, babies will often suck their thumbs, grab their own blankets, or bury their heads in a parent's lap when they see someone else in distress. They are trying to relieve their own empathic distress created by hearing or seeing someone in pain. They will also approach trusted adults to get a hug, to play an interactive game such as peekaboo or patty cake, or to tumble around on the floor. Although the concept of sharing and helping is not yet formulated in a baby's mind, parents can model such behavior and talk about how good it feels to do both, inviting the baby to join in ("Here's part of Daddy's cookie for you," "Can I have one of your strawberries?" "Can you hold Mommy's car keys?" "Thank you").

TODDLERS

Between one and two years old, children begin becoming aware of their own emotional states, the characteristics of those states, and the potential for acting on those states. Children at this age can tell if someone else is hurt or sad— they can read, albeit not always accurately, the physical and psychological states of other human beings. They will often attribute these same human characteristics to their stuffed animals or real pets. If you ask whether Big Bird is sad, your child might say yes, look sad herself, and put her toy in a "sad" posture. She will also take great glee in the dog running in circles with her because they are both "happy."

Toddlers are able to empathize—that is, they have the emotional capacity to effectively experience (be moved by) another person's emotional state and see that person's emotional state as separate from their own. Although they can see that the distress is separate from their own, they will often try to relieve that stress by doing what they know would relieve their own distress. Seeing Beth crying when her mom leaves the room, Jeff hands her his teddy bear. Since the bear is what comforts Jeff, he assumes it will comfort Beth. When Michael falls in the sandbox, Jill rushes to get her own mom to help him—even if Michael's mother is close by. Jill knows her mom would help her, so she must be able to help her playmate; she has no clue about the other mom's caring potential.

By the end of their second year, children already have the cognitive ability to roughly interpret the psychological states of others, the emotional capacity to effectively experience the other's distress, and a small but growing behavioral repertoire to attempt to alleviate the distress or pain of others. Since toddlers can roughly interpret the psychological states of others, they can tell by your body language, as well as by your words and actions, if they have failed to live up to your expectations. If a child is regularly humiliated or shunned or isolated or punished, he is likely to feel ashamed. This shame is not healthy guilt. Healthy guilt develops naturally in later childhood and is a part of the underpinnings of inner discipline and self-evaluation. Shame, on the other hand, is dependent on the perceived or real evaluation of others, especially of important adults in that child's life. Shame interferes with a child's ability to acquire the sense of self-control and agency that is so critical to a child's moral development.

Toddlers' play is still mostly parallel play, playing alongside and occasionally interacting with peers. It is also the time children declare "me," "mine," "myself" (as in "I'll do it myself"). Sharing is more accidental than planned, and the desire to help is interspersed with "no."

By age two, children are into make-believe and can spend hours playing house. If we listen and watch carefully, we will see our own actions and words mimicked. This is a wonderful—and at times disheartening—experience. Watching them rock the baby doll or feed the teddy bear, we smile. Listening to them tell the teddy bear that he will get a spanking if he doesn't finish all of his vegetables, we cringe. Hearing our words come out of their mouths with full inflection and feeling, we know, whether we like it or not, that our children are learning from us all the time.

It is at this age that children begin to develop an awareness of right and wrong. They become upset when they break a toy accidentally, but even more upset or even angry when someone has intentionally broken that toy. They cry when a sibling pulls the tail of the cat and the cat becomes distressed. The rudimentary awareness of justice and injustice shows itself when it comes to dividing up treats or toys. A toddler lacks the intellectual understanding of why an action is wrong: "Don't run into the street" and "Don't hit" to a toddler are both the same "don't." She doesn't yet distinguish between "because it is dangerous" and "because it hurts the other child."

PRESCHOOLERS

By three years old, children are able to discern another's inner states as being independent of their own. They can more accurately discern what might be of comfort or help to the adult or child in distress. Their repertoire of caring behaviors is growing and tends to be more appropriate to the situation.

It is at this age that comforting, sharing, and helping become staples in a child's interactions with adults, siblings, and peers. The more opportunities you can give your child to do all three, the more she begins to know herself as capable of caring, sharing, and helping: "You can fill the dog's water dish so he won't get thirsty." "I'll cut the peach so both you and Mark can have half." "Help me put the celery on the plates."

This is also the age at which children truly interact with their peers, thus the inevitable conflicts, selfish actions, and declarations of "That's not fair." It is time to actively socialize your child to consider others—their feelings, their needs, and their wants: "It hurts Sarah when you tell her she can't play with any of the toys. You don't have to give her your favorite doll, but you need to let her play with one of the others." "If you share your toy with Geoff, he can have fun playing, too." "Zev wants a turn on the swing, too." "It's not fair to hog the sandbox toys." "If you push him, he will fall down and cry." "She will be upset if you take her toy without asking first."

Interacting with peers helps kids at this age to begin to realize that others have claims, and that sometimes those claims compete with theirs. They also begin to learn the "rules" of social propriety, and simple rules for games. Don't be surprised or shocked if they bend the rules in their favor. It may disappoint you to see your child "cheating," but just as Hartley spoke of the past as a foreign country, in childhood, they do things differently. Children are just beginning to develop their own moral sense, and it will be several years yet before they develop the ability to knowingly cheat or to actively resist cheating. At this age they have trouble telling the difference between real and pretend, between a fantasy and an untruth to keep from getting in trouble. What we may deem lying is, to them, not even stretching the truth—it is the "make-believe truth."

By four years old, most children can adopt another's perspective—a critical milestone in being able to reflect on the impact of their own behavior on other people and to successfully come to the aid of someone in distress. Melissa shared her cookie with her peer "because he was hungry." This is the heart of altruism—doing good for another for the sake of the other. The spark that Hoffman wrote about has now developed into an empathetic proclivity that he calls an "ally within the child." It is this ally that enables us to use induction (teaching) as a part of discipline (as opposed to using punishment) to promote our children's prosocial behavior and reduce their aggression.

When children have to attend to the consequences of their actions (or inactions) for the target of their aggression, we are helping them to call forth their empathic distress and the beginnings of healthy guilt. Their transgressions, and subsequent follow-up with appropriate discipline, are seen as opportunities to create an ongoing script: transgression *plus* empathic distress at seeing someone in pain *plus* guilt from causing that pain *plus* discipline *equals* the possibility that the next time they are in a similar situation both their image of themselves as caring people and their memory of the guilt will preclude their responding in the way that precipitated the discipline in the past. It equals the *possibility*, not necessarily the *probability*, that a child will behave differently. It takes time and practice to develop a sense of internal discipline. It is developing this inner sense of discipline that is not dependent on external force, manipulation, or control that was the thrust of *kids are worth it! Giving Your Child the Gift of Inner Discipline*. It comes into play once again here in the service of our children developing their own ethic rooted in deep caring.

Children at this age are very concerned about fairness and justice, but their understanding of these concepts is beginning to expand. Justice might mean simple equality, or it might be related to more sympathetic factors ("He's hungry," "She doesn't have any toys," "He's sad"), or to more objective criteria ("He didn't follow the rules of the game," "She jumped two spaces instead of one," "I'm bigger so I get more"). Capitalizing on your children's concerns about fairness and justice and helping them apply these concerns to their everyday conflicts with peers opens them up to being more receptive to resolving their conflicts peacefully and justly. It takes example, guidance, and instruction from us to impart to our children that violence is an immature, irresponsible, and unproductive technique to resolve conflict, and that using nonviolent tools to resolve conflict is a mature and courageous act. But it takes involvement with their peers to make it real to them. Moving from solitary play, to parallel play, to interactive play, to cooperative play can only happen if children have opportunities to be with peers. The budding relationships that children have at this age with their playmates—learning to share toys, resolve conflicts, and cooperate in games and imaginary play—form the foundation for more lasting friendships in the elementary years.

ELEMENTARY YEARS

By the time they are six or seven, children are more intellectually capable of responding constructively and more emotionally capable of responding compassionately. They are more able to accurately identify what a person is feeling, to figure out or to speculate about what has caused the distress, and to see what the other person needs to relieve the stress. It is also at this age that children begin to separate moral issues (fairness and justice) from social conventions (clothing customs and etiquette).

Friendships develop, with all the emotional ups and downs that close interpersonal relationships create. Friendships between children provide unique experiences in the interconnection between the self and another that are on a more equal basis than in relationships formed by children with adults. But they don't just happen. We need to teach children how to be a good friend, not just to be sure to have friends. Good friendships are the foundation on which children can build more intimate relationships in the future.

Kids at this age learn not only to share toys and snacks, they learn to share friends. They learn to work cooperatively with groups of friends, and sometimes compete to be the "best" friend of a popular peer. As they grow older, kids begin to be more selective about the people they choose to befriend. As they become more selective, they may also tend to establish cliques or in-groups and out-groups based on stereotyping and prejudices. It is their ongoing experiences and learning at home that will either reinforce these stereotypes and prejudices or create a buffer against such intolerance and bigotry. Your child's internalized, emotionally charged sense of right and wrong will prove to be a valuable asset in her being able to stand up for another child and against an injustice.

Elementary-age children are less inclined to follow the rules formulated by adults if those rules would, in their own minds and hearts, violate caring and sharing and helping. Seeing her classmate in distress over a reading assignment he was struggling with, Jamie readily helped Jon, even though the teacher told Jon he would have to figure out the words himself. Steve helped Ben find his coat after the other boys had hidden it at recess. Both boys got a tardy slip for being late, but Ben didn't care—it was more important to help his friend. When Kathy was sent to bed without her supper because she talked back to her mom, Kathy's twin, Kelly, snuck some food for her to eat.

Children of this age have a greater understanding of "fair play." They understand that the rules of a game can be changed with mutual consent, and that right and wrong is not so black and white. They develop more fully an internal sense of pride or guilt that is not dependent on external affirmation or denunciation. A heavy reliance on bribes and threats or rewards and punishments to get children to "behave" can sabotage this development.

Eight-year-olds begin to balance justice with mercy, and are more willing to have more mercy on and judge less harshly those who express remorse or regret. It is at this stage that children begin to more fully comprehend how the Big I (intent) and the Three Cs (content, circumstances, and consequences) can change the nature of an act. They are capable of weighing which action would bring about the greater good and able to effectively balance competing claims. They can utilize their abstract thinking skills to discuss moral dilemmas, temptations, and ethical actions in their own lives, in the lives of people in the news, and in fiction and nonfiction literature.

Between ten and twelve, children show genuine compassion for people who have been dealt with unjustly or who live in unfortunate circumstances. They can care enough to want to relieve their suffering as much as possible, even though they don't know them personally. Given the opportunities to care and to share and to help—writing letters of protest and collecting money to free child soldiers, collecting canned goods for a food drive, reading to preschoolers, singing at the seniors' center, stuffing backpacks for children who have been affected by a flood half a world away—they construct more consciously their own moral code.

TEENS

Teens are on the cusp of being adults and even in the early teen years are capable of highly abstract reasoning and passionate convictions. They are emerging as unique personalities, with their own strongly held beliefs and values. They are quick to point out any insincerity, hypocrisy, or injustice at home, in their school, in their community, and in the world. They can drive you a bit crazy as they manage to call you on any indiscretion, no matter how slight ("Mom, that was a rude comment you made to my friend—you tell me not to be so judgmental," "Dad, you tell me to be honest with you but you don't tell Grandma that you smoke"). But that bit of crazy is an opportunity for you to show your teen that you can accept the valid criticism and demonstrate that you are willing to right a wrong.

Moving toward independence in all areas of their lives, they still need our modeling, support, and guidance. They need to see us behaving ethically in all areas of our own lives. They need to see us stand up and speak out against injustices, in the family room, the boardroom, the classroom, on the streets, or in the halls of government. (Yes, I was in front of the U.S. consulate in Toronto to protest the killing of men, women, and children in bombing raids in Iraq.)

Sometimes that speaking out requires from us a rebellion of sorts—that is, actively working toward changing a convention, tradition, or general practice. With the visible support and encouragement of their parents, a group of high school students confronted the school board on its refusal to support the removal of a team mascot that was both gender biased and ethnically biased. The arguments that the mascot had been around for several generations and that the alumni would not support a change did not bow the students. They created their own mascot and covered the offensive ones in the school gym. They printed T-shirts with the new symbol and convinced all the teachers and the principal to wear them to the next school board meeting. They held interviews with the media and put forth a strong ethical position that was hard to argue against. The mascot was changed—and so were the students. Emboldened by their success and energized by the cause, they decided to take on other entrenched biases they found in the local media and in their high school textbooks.

Given the opportunity to meet or study people who are vigorously involved in humanitarian efforts, teens can be energized to make a difference themselves without being bribed or threatened with "compulsorily volunteerism" credits. Shyrna Gilbert, a Toronto high school teacher, introduced her students to the organization Hope for Rwanda, which raises money for orphans in that African country. Years later, many of her former students are still actively involved in humanitarian efforts in their own communities and abroad. When asked, many of them attribute their own social activism in large part to the passion and concern demonstrated by their former teacher.

Kids who have nurtured their ability to be empathetic, sympathetic, and compassionate in the elementary years, who have developed a view of themselves as caring individuals, and who have developed a healthy anticipatory guilt are more likely to weather the teen years without compromising or grievously harming themselves or others. (Anticipatory guilt is a guilty feeling that precedes an act one knows would be unethical—breaking a promise, spreading a rumor, cheating on an exam, lying to get out of a date because someone else asked later.) When they view themselves consistently and over time as one who doesn't usually lie, cheat, or steal, hate, hoard, or harm, in moments of temptation, they can call upon that internal ethical self to help them resist.

Teens' close friendships tend to be more supportive, more intimate, and less competitive than those they had in the elementary years. At the same time, their groups of friends may be more cliquish and exert incredible pressure for conformity. Kids who were given opportunities to make lots of choices, decisions, and mistakes when they were younger will be better equipped than their peers to resist conformity that is harmful.

Dating brings a whole host of ethical and moral concerns, decisions, and responsibilities. All the caring and sharing and helping you did with your children from the time they were infants—including sharing age-appropriate information about their sexuality—all the friendships they developed, and all the opportunities they had to practice resolving ethical conflicts and solving ethical dilemmas will be of great service to them now. With their healthy sense of wonder and skepticism still intact during this time of raging hormones and simple questions that have complicated answers, your teens will wonder about falling in love, crushes, self-pleasuring, homosexuality, heterosexuality, intercourse, and issues related to wet dreams, periods, pregnancy, and birth, and all the ethical issues surrounding each one of these topics. The questions surrounding sex, values, intimacy, and commitment bring to the fore the necessity of having an ethic that is rooted in deep caring, one that is concerned not only with the "I" or the "Thou" but with the "I *and* Thou *and* We"—*and* the possibility of another "Thou." When their peers' beliefs, values, and sexual relationships and activities run the gamut from strict absolutism to "if it feels good" relativism, they will find they have a still-evolving but well established moral center of their own to draw on, and the comfort of knowing they can talk about sexual issues—the good, the bad, and the ugly—with their parents.

> Parents can only give good advice or put them on
> the right paths, but the final forming of a person's
> character lies in their own hands.
>   —ANNE FRANK, *THE DIARY OF A YOUNG GIRL*

Chapter 3

Our Worldview
and Why It Matters

The lessons in "right" and "wrong" are hard lessons—not swiftly accomplished by setting up as an objective the learning of some principle. We do not say: It is wrong to steal. Rather, we consider why it was wrong or may be wrong in this case to steal. We do not say: It is wrong to kill. By setting up such a principle, we also imply its exceptions, and then we may too easily act in authorized exceptions. The one caring wants her child to consider the act in its full context. She will send him in the world skeptical, vulnerable, courageous, disobedient and tenderly receptive. The "world" may not depend on him to obey its rules or fulfill its wishes, but you, the individual he encounters, may depend on him to meet you as one caring.
—NEL NODDINGS, *CARING, A FEMININE
APPROACH TO ETHICS AND MORAL EDUCATION*

Matthew's mother dropped birthday invitations into the backpacks of all of the boys in her son's grade two class—all of the boys except Jason, whom the birthday boy considered "wimpy." During recess Jason tearfully told his classmate Andrew about not being invited to the party. Andrew patted him on the back and told him not to worry, that he hadn't got an invitation either. Later that day, having heard about the party from Matthew's mom, Andrew's mother suggested that Andrew go shopping for a present. Andrew pleaded, "Please Mom, I don't want to go to the party. I can't go." He then explained that in an attempt to comfort Jason, he had not told him the truth.

Do you punish Andrew for lying? Do you make him go to the party? Do you suggest that Jason probably did something to deserve to be excluded? Do you tell Andrew how proud you are of him? Do you just let the matter drop because you don't know what to say or are too busy with your own concerns? Or do you talk with him about the dilemma he found himself in and possible options for now and in the future? Do you tell him how disappointed you are that Matthew's mother would be so willing an accomplice to her son's meanness?

How you answer reflects your way of understanding the world, your conception of morality, what you think makes a "good" person, and what is the "right" thing to do.

OUR FAMILIES, OUR WORLD

If we want children to resist [peer pressure] and not be victims to others' ideas, we have to educate children to think for themselves about all ideas, including those of adults.
—RHETA DEVRIES AND BETTY ZAN, *MORAL CLASSROOM,
MORAL CHILDREN, CREATING A CONSTRUCTIVIST
ATMOSPHERE IN EARLY EDUCATION*

In *kids are worth it! Giving Your Child the Gift of Inner Discipline* I discussed at length three kinds of families: the Brickwall, the Jellyfish, and the Backbone. We saw how each of these three families embodies a different approach to the everyday challenges of child-raising—mealtimes, bedtime, and household chores—that sets them apart from one another. What distinguishes these three family types is the structure that holds them together. This structure affects all of the relationships of the family: child to parent, parent to child, parent to parent, child to child, and the way the family as a whole relates to the outside world.

These three kinds of families also metaphorically symbolize our worldview. They provide a set of assumptions about human nature. These are the assumptions that inform our way of being in the world: our day-to-day encounters with others, our critical life choices, our religious views, our political stances, and our moral decision-making about what's right and what's wrong. Often we are unaware of the subtle and/or unconscious influence that these structures have on us in our day-to-day thoughts, feelings, choices, decisions, and actions—and more importantly, how they subtly and not so subtly influence the way we care for our children, the way we teach them about morality and ethics, and the way in which we present the world to them.

In his book *Moral Politics, How Liberals and Conservatives Think*, the renowned cognitive linguist George Lakoff analyzed the worldview of liberals and conservatives in the United States and postulated that the differences between the two come from different conceptions of morality and family life. He demonstrated that embedded in our language of ethics and morality are different models of the family—the

Parent Moral Models—each based on different assumptions about children, best practices of childrearing, and morality.

Your examination of the three types of families in terms of the Parent Moral Model in each will help you to identify things that are happening in your family that are helping your children become decent, caring human beings—and what might be getting in the way. The keys are becoming conscious of the messages you are giving your children, directly or indirectly, and becoming aware of the emotional and physical environment you are creating for yourself and for them.

BRICK-WALL FAMILY

> It was constantly impressed upon me in forceful terms
> that I must obey promptly the wishes and commands
> of my parents, teachers, and priest, and indeed all
> grown-up people, including servants, and that nothing
> must distract me from this duty. Whatever they said
> was always right. These basic principles by which I
> was brought up became second nature to me.
> —RUDOLPH HÖSS, COMMANDANT AT AUSCHWITZ

The brick wall is a nonliving thing, designed to restrict, to keep in, and to keep out. In Brick-wall families, the structure is rigid and used for control and power, both of which are in the hands of the parents. The building blocks—the bricks— that are cemented together to make the family are a strict hierarchy of power, an obsession with obedience, control, and order, and a rigid adherence to rules. Kids are controlled, manipulated, encouraged to conform, and made to mind through punishment—especially physical punishment—as well as bribes, threats, and rewards. Their feelings are seen as irrelevant or as a hindrance to becoming moral human beings; thus these feelings are ignored, ridiculed, or negated. Being good is equated with being obedient through the unreflective and immediate compliance with the commands and demands of the parent.

The Brick-wall family is in essence a dictatorship—perhaps a benevolent one, but a dictatorship nevertheless. Power in a Brick-wall family equals control, and it all comes from the top.

The parent's role is to protect, support, and teach right from wrong. The parent has absolute authority, enforces order, and must win any battle with children. Any questioning of the parent's authority demands immediate and painful punishment. J. Richard Fugate in his book on parenting, *What the Bible Says About Child Training*, reiterates this point: "The only issue in rebellion is will; in other words, who is going to rule, the parent or the child. The major objective of chastisement (that is, physical punishment) is forcing the child's obedience to the will of his parents." Another writer, Roy Lessin, offers similar advice in his book *Spanking:* "Obedience from children should be unquestioned; it should not be based upon how reasonable a command sounds to a child. A parent's directive does not have to be reasonable to the child in order to be obeyed." The child is to obey an order given by the parent, no matter how mistaken, misguided, or unreasonable, without question, without thought, without resistance, and without delay.

James Dobson, psychologist and director of Focus on the Family, uses the language of warfare when writing about breaking a child's will in his book *Dare to Discipline:* "The child may be more strong-willed than the parent, and they both know it. If he can outlast a temporary onslaught, he has won a major battle, eliminating punishment as a tool in the parent's repertoire. Even though Mom spanks him, he wins the battle by defying her again. The solution to this situation is obvious: outlast him; win, even if it takes a repeated measure." In *For Your Own Good, Hidden Cruelty in Child-rearing and The Roots of Violence,* Dr. Alice Miller describes this practice of coercion and cruelty under the guise of childrearing and refers to it as a "poisonous pedagogy." Dobson deems this practice necessary for the child's "own good"—although what is good about it is not explained because there is no need for explanation in such a family. What is forgotten, or perhaps never learned, according to Miller, is that a "lack of empathy for the suffering of one's own childhood can result in an astonishing lack of sensitivity to other children's suffering."

George Lakoff identifies a family structure that he calls the Strict Father Model. The Strict Father would be the head of the household in the Brick-wall family. This might be a father in the flesh, or in his absence perhaps a mother or other adult family member who is held in the sway of the Strict Father Model, either assuming the role herself or replicating with her children what was done to her in her family of origin.

In the Strict Father Model there are separate and strictly enforced roles for children to assume. Boys are trained to be daring, aggressive leaders. Defined in opposition to that which is identified as feminine, boys learn to repress any feelings of weakness and they fear appearing vulnerable

("Big boys don't cry," "You run like a girl," "Those who oppose me are 'girly-men'"). Boys are first obedient to the father, in order to become morally upright persons who, in turn, will be the heads of their own households, to protect and provide for their families. They are groomed to be powerful and successful.

Girls are trained to be followers. They learn to be obedient to their father in preparation for being obedient to their future husbands. Girls learn that their place in life is to be of service to their husbands, first, and then to be caregivers for their children. Any attempts to change this hierarchy or the roles inherent in it are viewed as wrong and bad. How could it be otherwise if the moral system of this model is right and good? And if this hierarchy and the roles within it are a part of this moral system, they, too, must be right and good—not to be tampered with or changed. Susan Moller Okin argues in her book *Gender, Justice and Family* that, historically, principles of justice and fairness have not been applied to family relationships. Instead, females have typically been treated unfairly by males in positions of power, influence, and privilege, who believe they have natural—or God-given—entitlements. One of the disturbing affirmations of these supposed entitlements can be found in *How to Rear Children* by the Reverend Jack Hyles:

> [A] girl ... must be obedient all her life. The boy who is obedient to his mother and father will some day be the head of the home; not so for the girl. Whereas the boy is being trained to be the leader, the girl is being trained to be the follower.... This

means that she should never be allowed to argue at all. She should become submissive and obedient. She must obey immediately without question, and without argument. The parents who require this have done a big favor for the future son-in-law.

When women and children are treated as less than or inferior to men in a culture, a man is more likely to act as a dictator both to his wife and to his children, and is less likely to respond in an empathetic way toward their feelings and actions. Since children are seen as sinful, willful, and defiant, any rebelliousness must be stopped and the willful spirit broken ("Stop crying or I'll give you something to cry about," "Don't you argue with me or you will find yourself on the short end of this long belt," "You keep smirking while I paddle you and I will paddle you until that smirk is wiped off your face"). Parents employ the tools of isolation, shaming, and grounding, on top of physical punishment or in its place, in an attempt to control children and "make them feel the pain" for whatever "wrong" they did ("Go to your room, right now," "How could you be so stupid?" "You are such a crybaby— no wonder no one will play with you," "What a sissy you are," "Shame on you for acting like a five-year-old," "Go away, we don't want girls who are mean to eat at the dinner table with us," "You're grounded for a week for answering back"). Subtler than physical force, these forms of punishment can still degrade, humiliate, and dehumanize children. Children learn to behave "appropriately" in response to the fear of getting caught and punished. Faced with domination, manipulation, and control by someone bigger and more powerful, children will respond in one of three ways:

Fright—the child is afraid to fight back or to make a mistake that will call down greater wrath from the parent;

Fight back—attacking the adult or taking their anger out on others who are smaller, weaker, or less powerful than them;

Flight—running away mentally or physically.

There are absolute criteria for what is right and what is wrong, rigid social rules, and codified courtesies. There are unyielding boundaries between what is good and what is bad. Rules are formulated dispassionately and impartially ("Don't hit your sister," "Don't lie to me," "Don't you dare talk to me like that," "Don't eat your peas with a spoon," "Good girls don't do that sort of thing," "You will not go to the dance"). Sometimes the rules are capricious and arbitrary, dictated for no other reason than to assert the authority of the parent to "make the children mind" ("Because I'm the dad, that's why," "There doesn't need to be any reason, so don't ask for one," "You will do those chores because I said so"). Failure to meet expected standards is "corrected" with some form of physical punishment—brute force, beating with switches or paddles, whipping with belts—the idea being that punishing the disobedient child will deter disobedience. When a child behaves obediently, she behaves morally. When a child disobeys, he is immoral. Children learn to do what they are told to do without questioning the person making the request or the demand, or questioning the purpose or consequence of the deed.

Children are considered morally weak, selfish, aggressive, and fueled by desires, emotions, and passions that will doom them if these are not reined in. Children need to be taught self-control, self-denial, and self-reliance to survive in a world that is viewed as an unsafe place with evil lurking around every corner. Parents alternate between the carrot and the stick to facilitate this learning ("If you go potty, you can have an M&M," "If you wet your pants, you will get a spanking," "If you are kind to your sister, I will take you to the mall," "You didn't share, so you don't get dessert tonight," "If you don't cry when you get the shot, we'll get you a toy at the store," "If you cry, I will leave you here at the doctor's to find your own way home," "If you keep pulling the dog's tail, you will have to go to your room," "Leave the dog alone or I will make him stay outside where you can't play with him," "If you don't smoke, I will buy you that computer," "If I catch you smoking, you will be grounded for a month," "If you don't date until you are seventeen, I will get you a car," "If you date him, you are no longer welcome in this house"). When push comes to shove, the parent will not back down or give in, resorting instead to bigger, better, more extravagant bribes and rewards to induce compliance, or bigger, harsher, more severe threats and punishments to force compliance.

The objective of these positive and negative control tactics is to compel or prevent actions and coerce children to behave in an adult-approved way. As a result, kids learn to do what they are told without question—*not because they believe it is the right thing to do*, but to get the reward or avoid the punishment. They become submissive, obedient, and compliant. Or they spend lots of time and energy figuring out if and how they can get away with something and not get caught.

Even when the bribes and threats, rewards and punishment appear to work, children who "do to please" have no deep understanding of the deeds they have done, they often have little or no commitment to what they are doing, and they fail to gain a genuine concern for their siblings or peers. Deeds are done merely or mostly for the payoff or to avoid the punishment ("Will I get credit for volunteering at the soup kitchen?" "I'll share my popcorn if I get to choose the TV program," "He'll ground me for a week if I don't get this done before he gets home"). Children are robbed of the opportunity to take risks, make mistakes, and question adults, for fear of losing the promised rewards or losing the parent's goodwill ("If I take that honors class I might not get an A and I'll lose out on getting the money Dad promised if I got straight A's"). Compliance is achieved at great cost.

If the rewards increase the probability that the child will do what the parent wants her to do, they also dramatically change the *why*, the *way*, and the *for whom* the task is done. In short order, coercion can bring about resentful obedience; it cannot create the desire to be good or to do good. Bribes and rewards and their flip side, threats and punishment, erode intrinsic interest and stunt children's ability to make healthy choices. They rob children of their creativity, autonomy, sense of well-being, and connectedness to those around them. These tools can give us compliance, but at the expense of creating less responsible, less resourceful, less resilient, less compassionate people who will "do to please," are praise-dependent, less generous, and less committed to excellence. These tools train children in selfishness and greed. Children ask, "What's in it for me?" not, "What kind of a person do I want to be?" Sharing and helping are calculated on the basis of shrewd self-interest ("If you let him play with your toy car, he might let you play with his new toy truck," "If you help her with the dishes, she will probably walk the dog for you"). Sharing and helping become commodities that can be bartered or bought at an ever-inflated price, and engaged in only when there is external pressure to do it or a profit to be had.

Nurturing and caring come with price tags as well—in other words, they are conditional. They are used to reward obedience and withheld to punish disobedience. In order to get affection or approval, children must do as they are told and are shunned when they don't ("If you clean your room, we will go see a movie together," "Touch my stereo and you will be in your room for the rest of the day," "Get out of here, no kid is going to talk to me like that," "Mommy doesn't hug boys who act like that," "Look what you have done to the family name—I am ashamed that you are my child," "If you ever get into that kind of trouble, don't bother to call home"). In a strange twist of logic, punishment is seen by the parent as an expression of love: "This hurts me more than you. I hit you because I love you enough to make you mind." "Spare the rod and spoil the child." When nurturing and caring are conditional, they are neither nurturing nor caring. Kids who must constantly earn their parents' approval or affection are so busy "doing to please" that they don't have the time, energy, or wherewithal to see themselves as competent, lovable, and caring human beings. They depend on others to affirm their worthiness or unworthiness.

In the Brick-wall family, it is assumed that life is a struggle for survival. With this in mind, competition is seen as necessary to affirm the proper moral order (i.e., establishing winners and losers, good and bad, strong and weak). Competition reinforces a strict us/them dichotomy. There are good people and there are bad people. The winners, the good, and the strong are on top; the others are losers to be avoided, adversaries to be defeated at all costs, and weaklings to be dominated and controlled. Moral strength equals self-control; moral weakness equals a lack of self-control. It takes self-control to be a winner. Parents encourage or force children to compete in order to get them to perform and excel ("Let's see who can get to the car the fastest," "Let's see who can carve the best pumpkin," "If you try harder, you can beat him out for the place on the team"). Rather than celebrating diversity and honoring differences, Brick-wall families rely heavily on the kind of competition that trains kids to see others as adversaries and obstacles to their own success. It is difficult to see an adversary as a potential friend. Competition can negatively affect kids' feelings toward their siblings and peers, stifling both the development of an innate ability to care and the desire to relieve another's suffering. Kids taught to feel good about their own success at triumphing over someone else do so at the expense of stifling the normal compassion they might have felt toward the one who lost. They prize self-assertiveness over a shared sense of solidarity with others. Kids are more likely to want to hang around with other winners, and not want to be seen with the loser, let alone ever come to his aid.

Competition is also viewed as practice for fighting the war against good and evil that is going on inside the child and in this unsafe world. Competition in childhood is seen as a way to "armor up" for the bigger battles to come. The argument that we must teach children to compete in order to survive in the real world would be valid if the world we want them to survive in were one of dog-eat-dog competition. If our goal is to raise them to survive in the real world and make it a better place, it would serve us well to examine this cultural attitude toward play, games, and organized sports, and reevaluate the premise that the world is a battlefield.

From the outside, a Brick-wall family often seems to be a close-knit family. But it is only a façade. It is held together by the absolute authority of the parent, and by strict rules enforced through the use of physical punishment, coercion, and intimidation. This authoritarian structure, bolstered by the supposed infallibility of the Strict Father, is inherently dishonest. Underneath the surface, masquerading as self-control and self-denial, lies a volatile mixture of anger, rage, degradation, and frustration, waiting to explode. Since children both witness and experience first-hand aggressive, antisocial behaviors exhibited by their parent, they often use those same skills to get their own needs met. Some seek others to control and dominate; others become highly judgmental; some store up their rage and resentment and let loose in acts of violence against themselves and their peers; some become compliant and apathetic, and thus easy marks to be led, manipulated, or dominated by any authority figure outside the family; and still others become so weakened that they have no inner resources to defend themselves or seek help. Children have a difficult time becoming responsible, resourceful, resilient, and deeply caring if they are controlled, manipulated, and made to mind, robbed of their autonomy and denied opportunities to make choices and mistakes.

Lakoff sums up the problems inherent in this model:

> Strict Father morality is not just unhealthy for children. It is unhealthy for society. It sets up good vs. evil, us vs. them dichotomies and recommends aggressive punitive action against "them." It divides society into groups that "deserve" reward and punishment, where the grounds on which "they" "deserve" to have pain inflicted on them are essentially subjective and ultimately untenable.... Strict Father morality thereby breeds a divisive culture of exclusion and blame. It appeals to the worst in human instincts, leading people to stereotype, demonize, and punish the Other—just for being the Other.

This absolute morality—the position that there are absolute and final answers to moral questions and dilemmas—leads to absolute intolerance and moral absurdities. Nothing fuels secular or religious extremism more than the belief that one is in possession of absolute moral truths. Once you believe you hold these truths, why be tolerant of those who would question or refuse to accept them? With no exceptions to absolutes, virtues can easily become vices, and one can too easily fall into the trap of self-righteousness and hypercritical moral judgment.

[O]ur lives indisputably have been influenced by the view that morality must be imposed, that ethical sense

must be, as it were, hammered into children, that the right thing to do is almost by definition the thing we would rather not do. If moral behavior is an externally imposed duty, we should not wonder that it becomes viewed as a chore and undertaken reluctantly.
—ALFIE KOHN, *THE BRIGHTER SIDE OF HUMAN NATURE*

JELLYFISH FAMILY

Children growing up in an atmosphere in which love and care are lacking or given with gross inconsistency enter adulthood with no ... sense of inner security. Rather they have ... a feeling of "I don't have enough" and a sense that the world is unpredictable and ungiving, as well as a sense of themselves as being questionably lovable and valuable.
—M. SCOTT PECK, *THE ROAD LESS TRAVELED*

The opposite extreme of the Brick-wall is the Jellyfish family. A jellyfish has no firm parts and reacts to every eddy and current that comes along. In Jellyfish families, structure is almost nonexistent; the need for it may not even be acknowledged or understood. A permissive, laissez-faire atmosphere prevails. In other words, anything goes; freedom becomes license. Different points of view are all seen as valid. The family is swayed by the conditions of the moment. It is assumed that children are at their best when left to their own devices. Children may become obnoxious and spoiled and/or scared and vindictive. Some keep their feelings under guard and spontaneity in check; others swing to the other extreme and become restless, uncaring, uncontrollable risk-takers.

In Lakoff's terms, the Jellyfish family is characterized by the Overindulging/Permissive/Neglectful Parent Model. This parent is found in—but is certainly not the head of—the Jellyfish family.

There are two different Jellyfish families. The first is created by the Overindulgent/Permissive parent who either doesn't know how to or doesn't care to create structure, consistency, and safe boundaries in the family. The Overindulgent/Permissive Parent might have come from a Brick-wall family and perhaps promised himself never to raise his children the way he was raised. Going from one extreme to the other, he is concerned about repeating the abuse he knew, but not knowing what to put in its place, he replaces it with very little. Or he might come from a family that was indulgent and permissive, and he is just repeating what he knows.

Both parent types tend to smother their children and rescue them from their own folly. Their children are sheltered from experiencing the unpleasant consequences of their own irresponsibility. Since such parents don't recognize their own needs, they can't tell the difference between what children merely want and what children actually need, with the result that they sometimes substitute lavish gifts for spending meaningful time with them. Their children's aggressive and sexual impulses are tolerated as "just the way kids are," or are actually encouraged by the parents, who are themselves self-indulgent and interested in their own pleasures. There are few limits and boundaries and almost no structure when it comes to mealtime, bedtime, chores, allowance, TV viewing, homework, and play. Children are allowed to make most of the choices and decisions about their behavior, with little if any guidance from the parent, regardless of whether those choices and decisions are appropriate to their age and abilities or not.

The other type of Jellyfish family is created by the Neglectful Parent, who physically or psychologically abandons her children, leaving them to fend for themselves. She has personal problems that keep her almost totally centered on herself. She may be incapable of caring for her children because of her own lack of a sense of self, or because of drug, alcohol, or sexual addiction, or a mental disorder. She may simply be too involved in getting her own life together to be concerned about the welfare of her children. The children may have all the material possessions they could want, or at the opposite extreme lack even the most basic necessities. They receive no nurturing, cuddling, or warm words of encouragement—only coldness. This deep sense of loss and grief shows itself not in bruises or broken bones, but in a broken heart—a hopelessness and despair. Children begin to believe that if anything is to get done, they must do it themselves; they can count on no one. They are unloved and abandoned. They learn to put aside or bury feelings of hurt, sorrow, and anger. They learn not to trust others and to lie and to manipulate people to get their basic needs met. They are often lonely and find it difficult, if not impossible, to be in a healthy relationship with others. Some behave as though they were cared for, putting up a brave but false front that requires an immense amount of energy to maintain.

The parents in both of these Jellyfish families use threats and bribes, punishments and rewards, but do so arbitrarily and inconsistently. One day a child is punished for hurting her brother; the next day she is rewarded for not hitting him all afternoon. The child who was hit begins to believe that he can count on nobody in the family to protect him. Home is not a safe place. His sibling doesn't learn to develop healthy ways to express her emotions and impulses. She learns there aren't always imposed consequences for her behavior, so she is willing to take her chances on not getting caught. Children learn ways to avoid getting caught doing something wrong and ways to get caught doing something good. It's all about getting caught—learning to work the system for the payoff—not about making and keeping friends, owning up to and fixing mistakes, or being kind or helpful because it is the right thing to do.

In this family, emotions rule the behavior of both parents and children. When emotions rule, it is difficult for children to develop their own inner voice that speaks to them before they act. They act without thinking about possible consequences and alternative responses. If anger is the most common emotion felt, children will begin to see hostile intent even in the benign mistakes of others. Often the parent expresses her own feelings and responds to her children's feelings in extreme ways. The parent will either smother the child or try to own the feelings for her. Smothered kids are unable to develop strong social skills, confidence, and self-awareness. If the parent rescues the child from feelings and situations, or makes excuses for her behavior, the child learns to be dependent on others to define her own feelings. She also becomes helpless at solving her own problems and is quick to lay blame on others.

It is the Jellyfish family, with its Overindulgent/Permissive/Neglectful Parent Model, that most clearly demonstrates the moral relativism so feared and denounced by the Strict

Father Model. By lumping this model with the Nurturing Parent Model and writing them both off as moral relativism, the Strict Father Model is able to maintain its either/or framing of morality. To do otherwise is to begin to chip away at the mortar of obedience that is so necessary to hold together all of the moral absolutes. The Backbone family, with its Nurturing Parent Model, doesn't just chip away at the mortar, it actually demolishes this entire structure of obedience and moral absolutes. In its place you will find an ethic rooted not in absolutes, principles, or virtues but in deep caring.

> Metaethical Moral Relativism (MMR): The truth or falsity of moral judgments, or their justification, is not absolute or universal, but is relative to the traditions, convictions, or practices of a group of persons.
> —CHRIS GOWANS, "MORAL RELATIVISM,"
> *THE STANFORD ENCYCLOPEDIA OF PHILOSOPHY*

BACKBONE FAMILY

> In order to develop, a child needs the enduring, irrational involvement of one or more adults in care and joint activity with the child.... Somebody has got to be crazy about that kid.
> —URIE BRONFENBRENNER, "WHO NEEDS PARENT EDUCATION?" *TEACHERS COLLEGE RECORD* '79

Backbone families come in many shapes, sizes, and colors. They don't come from any particular background or social stratum. They don't live in special neighborhoods. They aren't necessarily headed by older parents or by younger parents. They are not necessarily religious or non-religious, nor are they of any specific race or ethnic origin. They are characterized not so much by what they do or don't do as by how they balance the sense of self and the sense of community in all that they do. Interdependence is celebrated. Mutually supportive relationships rooted in deep caring and trust are the norm. Their physical, emotional, and moral environment is not rigid or unbending, not hierarchical or violent, nor is it cluttered with mixed messages or poor role models. Positive social behaviors are modeled and taught. Children are not perceived to be "born good" or "born bad," but are seen to be innocent—as capable of learning to care as of learning to hurt. Children are encouraged to explore, play, take healthy risks, and resolve conflicts assertively and peacefully. Mistakes are viewed as opportunities to grow, not as reasons for rebuke.

In the Backbone family you will find the family model that Lakoff identifies as the Nurturing (Nurturant) Parent. The Nurturing Parent is willing to put the long-term best interests of his children ahead of short-term compliance and docile obedience. This family provides the consistency, firmness, fairness, as well as the calm and peaceful structure needed for children to flesh out their own sense of self in relationship to other family members, peers, and the larger human community. Children know that they are deeply cared for and that they, too, are capable of caring deeply for others. Parents nurture their children's ability to be compassionate toward others, teach them to recognize the suffering of others, and show them effective ways to help relieve the hurt. A child's needs are acknowledged and met, freeing her from being preoccupied with them and allowing her to be open to others' needs, sorrows, and joys.

Nurturing Parents are emotionally available to their children, modeling appropriate ways to express the full range of emotions. Children learn to acknowledge and honor their own feelings. They also learn that they don't have to act on every emotion they experience. When their feelings are recognized and validated by their parents, children are less likely to become enmeshed in the feelings of their peers. Children need to see their own feelings as separate from those of their peers and to respond to their peers' sadness, fear, or hurt without becoming so sad, fearful, or hurt that they themselves are overcome or immobilized. They can see the pain, know what the feeling is like, and, with sympathy, respond in a way that will hopefully be helpful. When they have hurt someone, their parents communicate a deeply felt disapproval of hurting other people—a disapproval that is not only verbal but also emotionally charged.

Nurturing Parents don't demand respect—they demonstrate and teach it. They have a commitment to positive social values and communicate them directly, using reasoning that supports their children's own moral inclinations. They provide opportunities for their children to share with and help others. Children are spoken with, not to; listened to, not ignored. They learn to question and challenge authority that is not life-giving, as well as respect the true wisdom of their elders. They learn to be skeptical, open, and curious about themselves and the world around them. They learn that they can say no, that they can be respectful and be respected. What they say or do will not be taken lightly, dismissed, or shamed. They know that their preferences, their wants, and their requests will at least be considered, if not always accommodated. Given lots of opportunities to make choices and decisions with adult guidance—not adult commands or directives—children of Nurturing Parents are more likely to courageously step in when everyone else is stepping away, speak up when everyone else falls silent, and withstand criticism for their actions.

In the Backbone families that Nurturing Parents create, rules are simple and clearly stated. In establishing the rules, parents draw on their own wisdom, sense of responsibility, and perception of their children's needs. The rules are not for the purpose of making children mind adults; rather, they are intended to help keep children safe, healthy, and civil. In rooting their ethic—including rules—in deep caring, these parents demonstrate and teach their children what it means, when necessary, to abandon the rules in favor of caring. (Coming home late for curfew in order to take a classmate home who had no ride and would have had to walk. And because they knew their parent would be concerned, made a phone call home to explain the lateness—not to ask permission.) Manners are taught as social graces—rudiments of hospitality—that provide ways for children to engage creatively and constructively with siblings, peers, and adults.

Nurturing Parents constantly increase opportunities for their children to make their own age-appropriate decisions and to assume age-appropriate responsibilities. Thus, children learn to set their own emotional, physical, sexual, moral, and ethical boundaries.

Discipline and instruction are given in the context of a warm, nurturing, and deeply caring relationship with the child. When children are hurtful to siblings, peers, or pets, Nurturing Parents do not threaten punishment or sanctions; rather, they help their children to see and feel that what they have done is hurtful, give them ownership of the problem they created, give them possible ways to solve the problem and ways to heal the hurt; e.g., "Stop grabbing the dog's tail. It hurts him when you do that. Let me show you how to brush the dog gently. You can throw the ball for him to catch. I'll bet he would like that." Learning takes place in an atmosphere of acceptance and high expectation. Children are held to high standards of conduct, not to please their parents, but because their parents believe they are capable of being decent, responsible, caring people. They are taught to act with civility—that is, to treat another with the same dignity and respect they would want for themselves, even if they don't actually like the other person; to be willing when necessary to set aside their own wants for the greater good; to criticize; to hold accountable (but always with regard for the humanity of the other person); and to resolve differences respectfully. They learn to see their actions and inactions in their full context: intent, content, circumstance, and consequences.

Nurturing Parents establish consequences for irresponsible or uncaring behavior that are either natural or reasonable. At the same time they will be simple, valuable, and purposeful. There is no need for threats, bribes, rewards, or punishment ("You will need to replace the sweater belonging to your brother that you borrowed and lost," "The way you treated that new girl was mean and cruel; you need to fix what you did, figure out how you are going to keep that from happening again, and find a way to heal the rift you created—let's look at a decent and respectful way you can tell her what she is doing that is bothering you"). By being accountable for what they say and do—or don't say and fail to do—and being able to fix the problems they create, such children are less likely to place blame for their behavior outside of themselves. For serious transgressions and harm, parents help children work through the Three Rs of restorative justice: restitution, resolution, and reconciliation (see Chapter 5).

Love is unconditional. Nurturing Parents are there for the long haul—through all the good, the bad, and the ugly, and at all the ages and stages of their children's development. Children who are loved unconditionally are able to develop a healthy, secure attachment with a parent. This attachment allows children to further develop their own innate abilities to be optimistic, to persevere, and to be generous. Children who feel loved, wanted, and respected are more likely to be willing to celebrate differences and welcome others into their circle of caring. They are more likely to accept the advice and guidance of their parents and comply with family rules.

Smiles, hugs, and humor are given freely and abundantly with no conditions attached. Children see their parents enjoying their lives. By watching their parents give affection to each other, and by receiving loving and caring touches themselves, children learn that touch is critical to human bonding. They learn to master—not control—their own body functions, their sexuality, their impulses, and their attitudes.

Democracy is learned through experience. At family meetings, either informal or formal, all family members are aware of activities, events, schedules, and problems, and are invited to participate as fully as possible in planning activities, fixing schedules, solving problems, and resolving conflicts. Children see first-hand that their feelings and ideas are respected and accepted, and that it is not easy to juggle the needs and wants of all members of the family. As children grow in responsibility and decision-making abilities, they are trusted to take on more difficult and complex tasks and are entrusted with the care of siblings, elders, and family pets. They begin to comprehend what it takes to work together as a group, honor differences respectfully, and resolve conflicts peacefully. Their ability to perceive, see, or take others' points of view enhances their ability to be generous and helpful. As they experience a sense of belonging to a family and a community, they develop more mature beliefs about democracy and about legitimate authority.

Competency, cooperation, and collaboration are modeled and encouraged. Parents demonstrate the ability to do a variety of tasks and they help their children learn new skills. Chores are presented in such a way that they are meaningful to the children, useful for the family, and part of the harmonious order of the home. Children learn they can make a contribution and make a difference through working and playing with others. Play is seen as more than the absence of work, and it is not something that has to be earned. It is an opportunity to re-create and connect with others in the spirit of cooperation and acceptance. In his *Cooperative Sports and Games Book*, Terry Orlick speaks of the magic realm of play as a place where children experience personal growth and positive learning:

When children cooperate and collaborate with others in play activities, they learn to play with one another rather than against one another; they play to overcome challenges, not to overcome other people; and they are freed by the very structure of the games to enjoy the play experience itself. Children play for common ends rather than against one another for mutually exclusive ends. In the process they learn in a fun way how to become more considerate of one another, more aware of how other people are feeling, and more willing to cooperate in one another's best interest.

Children are able to master complex activities and intellectual pursuits through their interaction with caring adults, siblings, and peers. Recognizing that their children will be confronted with competition, Nurturing Parents attempt to raise competent, cooperative, decisive children who if they want to, need to, or are forced to compete, do it with a moral sense.

FROM ONE EXTREME TO ANOTHER

I am facing chaos everywhere I look. I want to go to church where they are going to tell me what's right, what's wrong, and there's no in between.
—AN UNIDENTIFIED WOMAN AT THE KANSAS
SCHOOL BOARD HEARINGS ON EVOLUTION
AND INTELLIGENT DESIGN, JUNE 2005

In terms of a moral worldview—a way of being, and of being with others, in the world—the three families (and Lakoff's three models) are at odds with one another.

The Brick-wall family, with its Strict Father Model, allows no "gray areas" in its vision of right and wrong. If all the world were a family, its duty would be to obey the father, whose word is law. This is a position of moral absolutism: the belief that there are absolute and final answers to moral questions and dilemmas. But the world is more complicated than this position suggests. "Always tell the truth," "Never steal," "Don't lie"—these unwavering dictates can cause one to become so wrapped up in the dogma as to lose sight of the complex events of a concrete life, and to fall into the trap of self-righteousness, hypercritical moral judgment, and intolerance.

The Jellyfish family, with its Overindulgent/Permissive/Neglectful Parent Model, demonstrates the other extreme, that of moral relativism.

If we accept that our only choices are a crude black-and-white moral absolutism or a wishy-washy, whichever-way-the-wind-blows moral relativism, then we are left with a rigid and divisive moral worldview. Our moral worldview is what shapes our beliefs, and the beliefs that we pass on to our children. And this either/or thinking is of no help to parents in raising children who can care deeply, share generously, and help willingly; who, to quote Nel Noddings, are "skeptical, vulnerable, courageous, disobedient and tenderly receptive," whom you can trust to meet you as *"one caring."*

It is, in fact, the Backbone family and the Nurturing Parent Model that most clearly exemplify the moral constructs that

I believe are the most helpful in creating an environment where our children can become "one caring." The Backbone family doesn't just chip away at the mortar of obedience. Instead it demolishes the entire structure of obedience and moral absolutes, and replaces it with an ethic rooted not in absolutes, principles, or virtues but in deep caring, with the supposition that deep caring may be informed by reason and will, principles and rules, but is neither controlled nor bound by them.

Being a Nurturing Parent isn't easy. There are no quick fixes, no edicts handed down from on high, no formulas or recipes for success, no pat answers, no absolutes to find a way out of a serious moral dilemma, no surefire remedies for whatever may be causing you or your children grief, no dogma to count on, no step-by-step manual.

If you aren't already one, *becoming* a Nurturing Parent is even more difficult—but not impossible. If you identified yourself in the other two models, or as a patchwork of all three, remember that you cannot change everything overnight. If you are currently bribing, threatening, or punishing your children, you can change your attitude, behaviors, and habits, but it will take time, a strong resolve and commitment on your part, and communication with your children. No matter what your history, it is possible to change your assumptions about your children, reevaluate your childrearing practices, and reframe your concept of morality. By knowing the possible alternatives and their potential impact on your children, you can mindfully and with a wise heart begin to create your own family model, one that will more readily enable you to teach your children how to think and act ethically.

Our humanity is caught up in that of all others. We
are human because we belong. We are made for
community, for togetherness, for family, to exist in a
delicate network of interdependence.
　　—ARCHBISHOP DESMOND TUTU, *NO FUTURE WITHOUT*
FORGIVENESS

WHAT DOES ALL THIS
HAVE TO DO WITH A BOY
AND A BIRTHDAY INVITATION?

Wisdom, compassion, and courage. These are the
three universal moral qualities.
　　—CONFUCIUS, *THE CONFUCIAN ANALECTS*

Andrew, the young boy who told his classmate he hadn't got
a birthday invitation either, was acting with wisdom,
compassion, and courage. Only one of the three family types
would likely have helped Andrew develop a personal ethic
rooted in deep caring.

It is not likely that a child from a Brick-wall family would
easily recognize the pain of the other boy, since he himself
has to stifle his own pain on a regular basis. Nor would he be
likely to attempt to ease that pain if he were to recognize it,
since his own disappointments are routinely ignored or
chastised. He might try to justify the birthday boy's choice
to exclude Jason, or blame Jason for doing something that
made Matthew not want to invite him.

If he were to comfort Jason and then tell his mom what
he'd done instead of making up another lie to cover up his
first, she would probably chastise him for lying, and tell him

it would be rude not to go to the party; he will go whether he wants to or not. Since she taught him never to lie, she might tell him that he will have to be punished for the lie when his father gets home. Or she might instead enter into a pact with her son not to tell the father, fearing that the father's punishment would be severe. (Yes, Jellyfishes can marry Brick-walls, and they do not a Backbone family make.) There is also a slim possibility that the mother would praise Andrew for telling her the truth. The praise would be a "moral credit" for telling the truth, and he would get his deserved punishment for telling a lie.

A child coming out of a Jellyfish family would probably be just as unlikely to recognize the pain of the other boy, having had his own pain ignored or dismissed. But if he did recognize the pain and tried to comfort the boy with the lie, his parent's response would be unpredictable. On a good day, Mom might abundantly praise Andrew for being kind, or try to "fix" Andrew's dilemma by helping him come up with another lie to explain to Matthew why he wasn't going to the party. On other days, she might see the whole event as no big deal, as just part of growing up, nothing to be concerned about. On a "down" day, she might tell Andrew that she doesn't want to hear about it, she has her own concerns, she is too busy to be bothered.

A child who has had to assume the caretaker role for his other siblings, because of his parents' neglect and disengagement, might readily recognize Jason's distress and respond with the lie. Having discovered that he must fend for himself, he would not have the encounter with his mother. She would be too concerned about her own life to worry about a birthday party. For this boy, lying would be doing what he felt was necessary to take care of another child—no big deal.

A child coming from a Backbone family is more likely to find himself in the birthday invitation dilemma. Having been deeply cared for and nurtured, Andrew sees himself as "one caring" and responds to the distress of his classmate. His parents have taught him that principles such as trustworthiness and truthfulness are very important to relationships, but they are not handed down as commands or hard-and-fast rules. They are important guides, and they help to simplify his life so that every time a situation comes up that begs for trustworthiness or truthfulness, he doesn't have to weigh the pros and cons ("Do I tell the truth or don't I?" "Do I keep my promise or break the trust?"). Seeing himself as a trustworthy and truthful person, he is not so easily tempted to lie or to break a promise. In fact, by age seven, he would feel pangs of guilt if his lie or betrayal of a promise were for his own comfort or convenience.

The principle of truthfulness is not an abstract, rigidly defined absolute. It is a principle *in service to deep caring*. If there comes a point at which this principle would denigrate, violate, or in any other way diminish deep caring, one chooses to lie in order to meet another as "one caring," as Andrew did. There has been no violation of deep caring, and I would suggest that there has been no violation of principle either.

Andrew's mother's response would be to meet Andrew as "one caring" as well. This is where a prescription of what to do gets sticky. I can only describe what I, as "one caring," *might* do if I were his mother. I would hug him and listen to his thoughts, his concerns, and his fears, and work with him to find a way out of this dilemma. I would also tell him how disappointed I am that Matthew's mother would be so willing an accomplice to her son's meanness, and wonder why her son was so adamant about not wanting to invite this boy.

Would I call Matthew's mom? Probably—as uncomfortable as it would be for me (caring is not about comfortable)—and I would tell her what happened and how upset I was that her actions contributed to putting my son in such a position. Would I listen to her? Yes. She might tell me I was a protective mother and that my son was wrong to lie. She might tell me her son had every right to invite whomever he pleased, and that there is nothing wrong with being selective with the invitations. She might agree that this was a mean thing to do and offer to invite the other boy immediately. Who knows? This scenario could take many twists and turns, depending on how each of us receives the other. There is always the possibility that she might hang up on me, and the saga would continue in a different direction.

LAYING THE GROUNDWORK

Each of us will be tested by encounters with cultures and viewpoints not our own; all of us will be refined in the fires of genuine engagement.
—CARDINAL BERNARDIN

Neither a rigid moral absolutism ("Because I said so …") nor a shifting moral relativism ("As long as I don't get caught …") will teach children how to care deeply, share generously, or help willingly. Neither will they provide the groundwork necessary to develop communities that will support, not destroy, that which nurtures children's innate ability to care. Growing up in a hostile, cold, punitive, indulgent, or neglectful household will not eliminate the possibility of a child becoming a decent human being; however, such environments will significantly reduce the chances of it happening. In creating a warm, caring, nurturing environment for our children, we get no guarantee that they will think and act ethically, that they will care deeply, share generously, help willingly, stand up for values and against injustices when the burden is heavy. But in such an environment, the possibility becomes more likely.

When the Nazis invaded Denmark in 1940, citizens of all ages united to form a strong resistance movement. One of those resistance workers, seventeen-year-old Preben Munch-Nielson, wrote an account of one of the daring rescues of Jews. In a note now posted at the Holocaust Museum in Washington D.C., he explained why he and many other Danes defied the Gestapo:

> You can't turn the back to people who need your help. There must be some sort of decency in a man's life and that wouldn't have been decent…. So there is no question of why or why not. You just did. *That's the way you're brought up.* That's the way of tradition in my country. You help, of course … could you have retained your self-respect if you knew that these people would suffer and you had said, "No, not at my table?" No. No way. So that's not a problem—you just have to do it. And nothing else.

Today various groups decry the diminished role played by institutionalized religion in our communities. Ethics committees are established to develop, adopt, and/or purchase "character education programs" in order to rescue our young from the "evils of secularism"—or even from their selfish, aggressive, and otherwise sinful, unpleasant selves. Political parties attack one another for subverting, undermining, and legislating against "family values." We are faced with the ever-present and expanding influence of the entertainment industry on the very fabric of our lives, and our children are venturing into the global neighborhood via the Internet, the cellphone, and the Blackberry. Can something as simple as an ethic rooted in deep caring make a positive difference? I believe it is the one thing that can.

This summer, in Rwanda, I met a woman who eleven years ago, in absolute desperation, begged an elderly Hutu neighbor to hide her eighteen-month-old Tutsi son. At risk of putting her own life in grave danger, and without hesitation, the old woman gently cradled the boy and said: "He's not a Tutsi; he's not a Hutu; he's a baby, and I am a mother."

The improvement of society does not call for any essential change in human nature, but chiefly, for a larger and higher application of its familiar impulses.
—CHARLES HORTON COOLEY

Chapter 4

Media: The Good, the Bad, the Ugly, and the Indifferent

And shall we just carelessly allow children to hear ...
tales which may be devised by casual persons, and
to receive into their minds ideas for the most part
the very opposite of those which we should wish
them to have when they are grown up?
                                    —PLATO, *THE REPUBLIC*

The fundamental nature of childhood is changing for
children growing up in a media-saturated world. No longer
do they spend countless hours playing open-ended games
or getting "lost" in adventures outdoors. Instead, they are
indoors multitasking their way through myriad electronic
media—watching TV, text-messaging their friends on their
cellphones, playing video games, and roaming the streets of
the Internet. A recent study of more than two thousand
eight- to eighteen-year-olds released by the Henry J. Kaiser
Family Foundation, *Generation M: Media in the Lives of
Children*, reports that, by doubling up on their media
exposure—watching TV while plugging in to the Internet;
text-messaging while listening to music—children pack
8.5 hours of media exposure into 6.5 hours a day, seven days

a week. Kids are plugged in, turned on, and tuned out for the equivalent of a forty-five-hour workweek, every week.

All forms of media have a profound effect on the way our children perceive the world. Since the media have the power to help define reality for our kids, the media also have a tremendous influence on who our kids become and what kind of world they actually inhabit. Media technology has become so powerful that we cannot afford to be laissez-faire about its consequences for our kids.

TELEVISION

Small town dad disarms chainsaw wielding
psychopath ... with skillful use of the remote.
—AD COPY FOR PAUSEPARENTPLAY.ORG

The rapid development in technology has had some positive consequences, allowing even young children to have access to people, cultures, and events from all over the world. This in turn helps build a global understanding and cultural awareness that is critical to breaking down barriers of ignorance and prejudice.

Children as young as three and four can travel the world with Sesame Workshop's *Global Grover,* learning about cultures, languages, and lifestyles of other children very different and yet very much like themselves. From this furry Muppet children learn not only to be respectful of differences but also to see the similarities, the joys, the sorrows, and the struggles that connect them to each other. History programs, nature shows, and travel channels give children of all ages a perspective and knowledge often not found in their textbooks, providing them with more up-to-date information and different perspectives on the subject matter.

In their article "Raising a World-Wise Child and the Power of Media: The Impact of Television on Children's Intercultural Knowledge," Ellen Wartella and Gary E. Knell write about the attempts to "harness the power of television to transcend physical and cultural boundaries, to influence lives, and to prepare children to flourish and learn in our ever connected world." Noting that *Sesame Street* is broadcast in more than 30 languages and reaches 120 countries, they point out its power to promote global awareness and mutual understanding:

> The South African production, *Takalani Sesame*, attempts to contribute to the educational goals of humanizing and destigmatizing people with HIV/AIDS through its five-year-old Muppet character, Kami, who is HIV-positive…. The Egyptian *Alam Simsim* … addresses that country's critical need to bolster education of girls through Khoka, a girl Muppet who aspires to succeed in a myriad of professions … *Sesame Street* has also begun work in areas plagued by ethnic and religious strife, such as Israel, Palestine, Macedonia, and Cyprus.
>
> In South Africa, research has confirmed that children who watched *Soul Buddyz*, a television series for children eight to twelve years old, had an easier time discussing such sensitive issues as race, gender, and disability.

Through media, person-to-person dialogue can take place in a virtual world that brings people from the far reaches of the earth into the same virtual chat room. Students are no longer restricted by time and space as they collaborate on scientific research with peers and scientists around the physical globe. Virtual schools offer advanced classes and other hard-to-offer courses that connect kids in hard-to-reach places with the rest of the world. In some schools in Kenya, children have no textbooks. Instead, they read stories, perform research, and do math on hand-held electronic devices that can be instantly updated.

The media *can* be used as an international educator, as a way to tune in to the world. It can also provide a way to tune out for a brief respite from everyday life and demands. But too much media involvement and too little "real life" social interaction and engagement stifle the development of social skills necessary to form healthy relationships. Much of the programming intended for our entertainment offers no modeling of civil behavior, and falls far short of showing us how to care deeply for one another. At the end of the first season of *Survivor*, one of the participants told another, "If I were ever to pass you in this life again, and you were laying there, dying of thirst, I would not give you a drink of water. I'd just let the vultures take you, and do whatever they want with you, with no ill regrets."

Caring deeply, sharing generously, and helping willingly are constantly butting up against messages of materialism, self-centered gratification, and gratuitous violence (often combined with sex), as well as unhealthy attitudes about girls and women and about relationships. Crude, raunchy, cruel, violent images and lyrics prevent the nurturing of empathy and respect, two critical elements of civility. Teachers have reported an increase in "mob mentality" among kids who routinely watch the "trash TV" talk shows that set out to provoke lively, and sometimes violent, confrontations. Hoping to provoke a peer to lash out, students gang up and taunt her unmercifully with vile comments about her looks, behavior, sexuality, and intellectual ability. So much for the school's thirty-minute character education lesson on the virtues of empathy, compassion, and respectful language. The television is a far more pervasive instructor. Humor, even in many children's cartoons, is usually not lighthearted, clever, or benign; nor is it intended to get everyone to laugh. Too often it takes the form of humiliating, cruel, demeaning, or bigoted comments thinly disguised as jokes. Laughter is directed at the person who is the butt of the joke. In an interview for *Newsweek*, the comedian and activist Bill Cosby said, "I do miss the days when comedy wasn't mean, when jokes weren't at other people's expense and you used profanity rarely. Getting people to laugh without being vulgar is the creative process at its best."

While teaching the difference between satire and sarcasm, I asked high school students to watch three of their favorite shows and write down every humiliating, cruel, bigoted comment that was thinly disguised as a joke and had a laugh track under it. One student came back the next day and said he couldn't write fast enough. Students were amazed at the number of these "jokes" they were exposed to in such a short period of time. That one homework assignment helped them to watch and listen more critically in order to discover the various ways humor is used in media and in their own everyday interactions, to discern which humor was harmful, and decide how each one of them could respond to such humor in the future. But the lesson, weighted against the onslaught of media messages, can't be just a one-day activity. It must become an ongoing dialogue with our children.

Many popular shows, movies, songs, and videos promote a "no limits, no boundaries, if it feels good, do it" ethic. Difficult moral dilemmas and everyday decisions are lumped together as just some of life's choices you get to make. Should I have cheese pizza or pepperoni? Do I cheat on my girlfriend or don't I? Is it really stealing if I just download a few songs? Think about your twelve-year-old deciding if it is right or wrong to spread an ugly rumor about a classmate after experiencing a steady diet of reality shows and sitcoms.

In media, people are often divided into the "bad" and the "good"—them and us. Various minority groups are portrayed in stereotypical fashion, and often in a negative light. It is almost impossible to develop the ability to walk in another's shoes, respond compassionately, or see someone as an equal when they are "not one of us."

In terms of consequences, there is no correlation between real-life violence and unreal media violence. Imitating wrestling moves he saw on television, a twelve-year-old killed a six-year-old neighbor. He had no clue that such a move could hurt anyone, let alone kill. A boy who shot a classmate was shocked that the other boy would be in such pain and that he would actually bleed so profusely. In the media there are often no negative consequences for perpetrators of violent acts. If the perpetrator is viewed as a "good guy," violence is actually cheered and rewarded. Rarely is remorse shown. Even more rarely does a violent program send any kind of anti-violence message.

> The medium is the message. This is merely to say that the personal and social consequences of any medium … result from the new scale that is introduced into our affairs by each extension of ourselves or by any new technology.
> —MARSHALL MCLUHAN, *UNDERSTANDING MEDIA*

NOT EXACTLY THE SOUND OF MUSIC

> Despite my fear and loathing, I began to listen more closely to songs spanning the continuum—pop, heavy metal, rock, rap, alternative, industrial—and to discuss with my young wards what drew them in. I saw, just as Dylan spoke what was in my heart in the '60s, some lyrics of these songs give voice to a generation…. More importantly, once I was actually willing to listen to their music, even as we argued over the destructive messages of their lyrics, teenagers trusted me more. In turn, they allowed me a fuller glimpse into their universe.
> —DR. RON TAFFEL, *THE SECOND FAMILY: DEALING WITH PEER POWER, POP CULTURE, THE WALL OF SILENCE—AND OTHER CHALLENGES OF RAISING TODAY'S TEENS*

The lyrics of the songs your kids are listening to through the earphones of their iPods will give you a "fuller glimpse into their universe." Watching your kids bopping around the kitchen, moving to the latest downloaded song, you may have no idea what they are receiving into their minds. Kids will often say that they don't listen to the words of songs. Don't believe it for a minute. Watch them mouth the lyrics to their favorite tunes.

It is not by accident that parents and teachers sing nursery rhymes and use music to teach the ABCs. For infants, music is a form of communication that comes before and transcends spoken language. A lullaby sung by a warm and caring parent enhances the bonding experience with the baby. This in turn contributes to the development of trust that is critical to enabling children to know their parent as caring, themselves as cared for, and as early as toddlerhood, as one who can care for others. Nursery rhymes invite social interactions with both adults and young peers. Who can resist "Patty Cake" or "Ring Around the Rosie" with a smiling toddler?

Early childhood musical games help children learn the rudimentary social skills necessary for caring, sharing, and helping one another. Playing those miniature drums, cymbals, and horn your (single and childless) brother gave your daughter for her birthday helps her to develop confidence in her ability to "make your own kind of music." Since she has more than one instrument, she can share her birthday gift with her peers, and together they can create a lovely cacophony, each contributing their own talents to the group. These activities become important parts of the foundation for building a strong sense of self in community.

Aristotle noted that there seems to exist in us an "affinity to musical modes and rhythms." The ancients felt that music could help tune the soul to the rhythms of a "good life." Playing certain kinds of music can calm colicky babies and cranky adults. Other pieces can bring a heaviness to your heart, or rouse you to march, or cause you to weep.

Music can also call forth powerful memories: the song that was "our song" reminds us of a first love; your grandmother remembers a story from the 1930s because of a tune she can sing by heart, even if she can't remember that you visited her last Sunday; a favorite lullaby from babyhood soothes a five-year-old after a bike accident.

Music can attach itself in our minds to convey powerful emotional meaning to thoughts or actions that have no direct correlation to the music itself. Commercials exploit this with popular lively music to sell a product. The tune sticks in the mind and becomes associated with the product. Coca-Cola paired its product with video from all over the world and the song "I'd Like to Teach the World to Sing." Hear song; think Coke; feel good.

Music can be used as the cord that connects and binds people to one another. This connection, as any other, can be used for good or bad.

Music can help solidify a group, create a deep sense of community, and join people together for the benefit of that community. Choral music, marching songs, theme tunes, ballads, folk songs, wedding hymns and funeral dirges, soundtracks for movies, school chants, and national anthems arouse or comfort individuals as they share in a communal event. Folk songs and spirituals were co-opted to energize people in the fight for civil rights.

Music also can be used to solidify a group of people to work against the common good of the larger community, or to energize them to attack a group targeted for exclusion or harm. The Southern Poverty Law Center put out an alert in late 2004 on the center's tolerance.org website about a Minnesota-based White Power record company distributing over 100,000 hate music CD samplers with mainstream appeal to white teens, aged thirteen to nineteen, "not to just entertain racist kids but to 'create them.'" As part of Project Schoolyard USA, the CDs were given away on school campuses throughout the United States and Canada and, thanks to the Internet, passed along to friends throughout the world like some kind of virus to eat at the hearts and minds of kids. According to the group distributing the CDs, Panzerfaust Records (a company now apparently out of business), the CD targets white kids who are sick and tired of what it calls "failed social experiment of multiculturalism" or of living in "dirty, dangerous, and foreign" neighborhoods. The songs include racist, hate-filled lyrics.

Mark Potok, director of the Southern Poverty Law Center's Intelligence Project, commented that "white power music has proven to be the most effective recruiting mechanism devised by the radical right.... [P]eople who have come out of this movement have said that this music was, by far, the single most important factor drawing them into the movement." And you were worried about the rap music with the mature rating that your child wanted to buy.

Asking kids to examine TV shows for humiliating, cruel, bigoted comments thinly disguised as jokes is one thing. Asking them to evaluate their CDs, DVDs, and MTV is quite another. They are not heavily involved *personally* in the excuses, such as, "They are only joking about raping and pillaging—nobody takes that seriously" or "It's only simulated sex, it's not real." (And you wonder, at that point, how they would know the difference.) "Die, Die, Die, Pig,

Die!" the kids argue, is simply shedding light on the dark
reality of ghetto life. There is a failure on their part to make
the connection that attacking violence with more violence
will only beget even more violence. Denouncing police as
"pigs" goes a long way toward dehumanizing the officers.
Once the target is objectified, dehumanized, kids can do
anything to it and not feel any shame or compassion.
They're killing a pig, not a person.

As powerful as visual cues and music are independent of
each other, combined they pack a tremendous punch. The
final product reinforces a message and enhances learning
and recall. Add the emotionally charged climate that the
new product creates and you have an intense learning labo-
ratory right there in the living room.

MTV founder and chairman Robert Pittman knew what
he was doing when he combined music and video to create
the phenomenon that would impact youth culture on an
international scale. He understood that teens "watch, do
their homework, and listen to music all at the same time."
"The only people who can understand the new way to use
that television set are the people who grew up on it…. They
will accept almost anything over that screen." When asked
about the influence MTV has on teens, he said: "At MTV
we don't shoot for the fourteen-year-olds, we own them."
He knows that our kids will listen, watch, and learn.

> Music has the power of producing a certain effect on
> the moral character of the soul, and if it has the power
> to do this, it is clear that the young must be directed
> to music and must be educated in it.
> —ARISTOTLE, *POLITICS*

VIDEO GAMES—FUN, FANTASY, FEAR, AND HATE

If we are forced, at every hour, to watch or listen
to horrible events, this constant stream of ghastly
impressions will deprive even the most delicate among
us of all respect for humanity.

—CICERO

Just as there are good movies and television shows, there are some fun fantasy video games—a good example is *MYST,* one of the best-selling games in the industry—which invite kids into a world that requires them to solve a mystery or accomplish a goal. With the incredible growth in the complexity and challenge of video games, there is much to be said about the ability of such games to draw kids into an intricate system where they learn the rules by interacting with fantasy characters, other real-life players sitting next to them on the couch, or an anonymous player at another computer or network a world away. Hand-eye coordination, quick thinking, cooperation, imagination, and problem-solving skills can all be strengthened and enhanced by playing video games. *SimCity* challenges kids to build their own virtual city. The dilemmas presented involve real-life quandaries and invite kids to create thoughtful and caring solutions. *Civilization* challenges kids to build a civilization from the beginning. Kids can work together to figure out ways for people to survive and coexist, making choices that have both intended and unintended consequences. All of these games reinforce the Big I and Three Cs that kids draw on in their everyday life to make ethical decisions.

There is another side to this electronic world our children are drawn to. Many video and computer games invite kids into a fantasy that requires little more than quick, aggressive, violent responses to perceived threats. The video culture of such violent fantasy seduces many emotionally vulnerable children. When they are saturated with vivid media images glorifying violence as the legitimate solution to problems and they practice these same acts of violence, they fail to learn or practice peaceful conflict-resolution skills. When they repeatedly play point-and-shoot video games that portray other people as adversaries, as prey, or as targets, they become desensitized to the act of shooting human beings, and the natural inhibition to killing people is broken down. The Simon Wiesenthal Center, which keeps track of hate websites, released a report in April 2004 that noted a surge in the number of online games that allow children to "shoot" illegal immigrants, Jews, and blacks.

In his article "Culture Quake" published in *Mother Jones* magazine, Paul Keegan describes the game *Quake III:*

> [It] gives you only a few seconds to enjoy the medium before you get the message…. As you drop hundreds of feet through space, you notice other inhabitants milling about on the landing platform below. Being a friendly sort, you approach them. Big mistake. They open fire. Reflexively, fearfully, you begin to shoot back. Heads and arms start exploding. In this magical environment, only one form of social exchange is permitted—kill or be killed. The images this astonishing new technology is most often called

upon to render so lovingly are rivers of blood and chunks of torn flesh.

Reflexively, fearfully—note there is no time for reflection. Playing enough games like this over and over again, kids will be less tempted to assume the best of strangers they meet. It will be "smarter" to assume hostile intent in the behavior of peers who are not in their own circle of caring.

In a British study, fifty boys were observed playing a nonviolent video game while fifty other boys played a violent video game. Both groups were then shown nondescript, ambiguous photographs. The boys who had played the violent video games gave more hostile descriptions of the pictures than those who had played the nonviolent game. It seems that playing the violent games actually contaminated their thinking and their emotional responses. They saw hostility where none existed. A German study of grade eight students concluded that those who played violent video games were more likely to condone physical aggression in real-life situations. A Minnesota study of more than six hundred students in grades eight and nine showed that children who play more violent video games see the world as a more hostile place; they get into more fights with peers and into more arguments with teachers.

When a child repeatedly plays violent games, his brain creates neural pathways that connect violence with pleasure and rewards. The "mirror" neurons in the cortex of the brain fire whether a child performs the action or merely sees the action performed by someone else. These neurons in turn form connections or pathways to the emotional center of the brain. The neural circuits that are created are thought to be the basis of an empathic response. Therefore, if a child playing a video game continually causes a character to brutalize or kill another character, and in turn the child feels excitement or thrill rather than sadness, sympathy, or fright, when he then sees a real peer being hurt or bullied by someone else he is more likely to join in the "fun" than come to the targeted child's rescue. Throw in getting a reward in the game for maiming and killing, and you get a child more willing to participate in violent activities if he is promised some of the bounty, or awarded higher status in a group of his peers.

Kratos, the protagonist of the action adventure game *God of War*, is smart, cunning, strong, and mean. He is out to save Athens in exchange for the gods' promise of forgiveness for his cruel and heinous past transgressions. There are some ingenious puzzles that must be solved and the storyline is intriguing. While solving these puzzles and following the storyline, kids can spend hours making Kratos perform brutal acts. The brain is busy making connections to the emotional center as kids are vicariously maiming and killing. The game does not allow kids to save people but will give them a "health bonus" for killing them. Imagine the neural connections being made in the brain when the gamer drags a caged soldier to his doom while he begs for his life.

A popular game with teen boys, *Grand Theft Auto III* invites kids to kill police, blow up their cars with bazookas, then machine-gun others and hear them scream. In this virtual reality, kids can go on to pick up a pair of prostitutes, spend time with them in a car, and then kick and beat them on the sidewalk—all these actions earning the player extra points. As reported in the Kaiser Foundation study,

65 percent of children in grades seven through twelve have played the controversial video that is rated for mature audiences (over age seventeen). Controversy surrounds the latest version, *Grand Theft Auto III: San Andreas*. A Dutch techie wrote a code that can be downloaded over the Internet. That code acts as a key to unlock graphically explicit sexual images that are hidden inside the game. Both the code writer and the producer of the game said nobody should be alarmed because the game is "not a game for young children, and is rated accordingly." If 65 percent of teenagers have played *Grand Theft Auto III*, how many do you think—considering all the hype and media attention about the code and the sexually explicit content—will spend hours playing this latest edition, bonus features included?

All video games offer nonstop stimulation. It is a sad commentary that this "Generation M" finds *comfort* in such stimulation. To be still is to be bored and uncomfortable. One eleven-year-old kept his Game Boy on his bedside table so that if he woke in the night, he could play the stimulating game, in his words, "To soothe myself."

There is no denying the addictive quality of the games. Twenty-two freshman students at a New York university flunked out due to "video game and Internet addiction." Kids forego watching a real basketball game to play the latest *NBA Live*, where they aren't just watching the game, they are controlling it—for hours on end. They wolf down dinner without saying a word so they can retreat into their rooms to play the fantasy game *Warcraft*. Four-year-olds log onto the Sesame Street website with their own passwords and play games that teach them to read and write and count and play with their playmates. If only they would occasionally shut down the computer and play with their live playmates down the street.

A point of view can be a dangerous luxury when substituted for insight and understanding.
                    —MARSHALL MCLUHAN, *THE GUTENBERG GALAXY*

INTERNET

Are we creating kids hooked on instant gratification? With no sense of consequences for their actions? Who don't know the difference between what's private and public, and who forever are in search of an audience? Kids who don't take deadlines and commitments seriously because they are in perpetual communication?
          —ANDREA GORDON, "WIRED, LIKE TOTALLY. TEENS
          DEPEND ON VIRTUAL WORLD TO COMMUNICATE
          AND EXPLORE THEIR IDENTITIES," *TORONTO STAR*

Internet: The "Net"—a name given to the worldwide collective of interconnected computers and computer networks. The Internet is the one media tool that can give instant access to the good, the bad, the ugly, and the indifferent. It can be an amazing tool when it is used appropriately to seek information from an online dictionary or medical database, to compose and share stories, or to correspond with cyber-pals a continent away. It can also be used to destroy the reputation of a classmate through the spreading of an ugly rumor in cyberspace. A predator looking to take advantage of a young girl's naiveté to stalk her can use it. It can be used to post on a website a morphed picture—taken with a cellphone camera—of a large boy suiting up in gym class. When he comes home from school he will be faced with hundreds of mocking e-mails.

Connecting to the Internet is like opening the door to a new—and vast—city. Some parents look at the ugly and absolutely scary stuff out there and refuse to let the Internet be a part of their family life at all. Some rigidly control availability of the computer, access to different sites, and time spent on the Net, regardless of the age, ability, sensitivities, and needs of their children.

Some parents are so ill informed and have so little desire to be computer literate that they allow their children to roam any and all streets, back alleys, and freeways of the Net. And if their kids should stop in at a chat room, heck, it's only a place to chat, just like stopping at the corner coffee shop. Then there are parents who know how ignorant they are and make an effort to learn at least as much as their young children know, and more—especially the parts about Net safety and Net etiquette. They realize that the Net is here to stay, and that teaching children to use it to their advantage, to get the most out of it, and to be safe requires the same tools that other communication and relationship skills require.

If you are reading this book, I trust you are among the parents who want to make the most of the Internet for themselves and for their children. The first step is to get all the up-to-date information you can. There are many good books on taking your kids online, protecting them in cyberspace, and negotiating the Net. I recommend you browse your local bookstore, talk to educators and other parents, and, if you can, explore the Net for resources. When your child acquires a screen name and password to use IM (instant messaging) and to enter chat rooms, many new neighborhoods open to them. Do you know them?

Just as you introduce new responsibility and decision-making opportunities in other parts of your child's life, and decrease limits and boundaries as they demonstrate the ability, confidence, and competence to be responsible, resourceful, and resilient people who know how to act with integrity, civility, and compassion, so, too, do you teach your children to live in the Net neighborhood and to navigate the roads. In his book *Growing Up Digital*, Don Tapscott explains the inherent benefits of the Net: "Internet connections give kids control over not only their keyboard, but over the feedback they receive from their social context.... Children do not just observe and receive information, they participate and create online. They inquire, discuss, investigate, play, fantasize, debate, they seek and they teach, they make value judgments at every turn."

Because I believe children should be taught how to think critically and not just taught what to think, I don't advocate loading down your computer with a Fort Knox protection system of blocking devices. In the early years of exploring the Internet, just as with exploring their own neighborhood, young children should be supervised while playing on the world wide web, with you giving advice, suggestions, and tools for dealing with unexpected intrusions. As kids get older, they can be trusted to handle the Net appropriately, as you continue to teach them such skills as how to evaluate world wide web resources with a critical eye, how to deal with someone who flames them (the same way they would deal at home with an in-your-face-bully), and what to do if they ever feel uncomfortable in a chat room. You can teach them to think before they hit the send button, and to refuse to participate in sharing private information online or sharing illegal software.

Unauthorized downloading of music files has become commonplace among teenagers—it's easy, it's convenient, it's illegal, and it's unethical. Would your child feel as comfortable going into a record store and walking out with a CD without paying? Does he feel it's easier to justify on the basis that all his friends are doing it? Does the fact that his friends would ridicule him for *not* doing it too make it all right? If the likelihood of being caught with illegal down-loads is roughly comparable to finding a needle in a million haystacks, is it okay for him to take his chances and go ahead? Just because he can, doesn't mean he should. There are opposing points of view as to the balance of benefit versus harm to the music industry that follows from illegal downloads, and these are valuable discussions to engage in with your child, but they don't change the fact that down-loading without paying is unethical. In addition, there are legal and ethical avenues for music downloading (iTunes is a popular one, at ninety-nine cents per legal song download) that you can point your child toward.

It is possible to lie, cheat, and steal while on the Net, just as it is possible to lie, cheat, and steal in your own neighborhood. If fear of getting caught is what holds kids back from lying, cheating, or stealing in their own neigh-borhoods, they will have fewer inhibitions to keep them from doing the same on the Internet, because the Internet gives them a certain amount of anonymity and a sense that they are invisible. Teaching kids from an early age to do the right thing because it is the right thing to do helps them to develop a personal moral code that is internal instead of external. This internal personal moral code will serve your children far better than your futile attempts to be a 24-7 monitor of Internet activities.

John Katz wrote a column entitled "The Rights of Kids in the Digital Age" for *Wired* magazine. He suggested that

> blocking software deprives children of the opportunity to confront the realities of the new culture: some of it is pornographic, violent, occasionally even dangerous. They need to master those situations in a rational, supervised way to learn to truly protect themselves. Blocking software gives the illusion of control. It doesn't ensure safety since sophisticated evildoers will circumvent it even more quickly than kids. And it doesn't teach citizenship in the digital world.

Far better you stay close, both physically and psychologically, as your child is learning to explore the Internet. As she grows older, still be close in terms of being aware of what she is doing on the computer and the amount of time she is spending on it. Get familiar with her web buddies as you would her school friends. Find ways to keep the lines of communication open, and opportunities to talk together about life in general and her friendships in particular. If she can share the good, the bad, and the ugly with you, and you've taught her how to navigate the Net and what to do, then she will be far better equipped to handle any situations that might come up. Remember, you trust her—it's some others who are on the Net that you don't trust.

Children whose parents are involved in their lives, who keep listening and talking with them, who know where they are, what they are doing, and who they are doing it with are less likely to get into trouble in their own neighborhoods, at school, or on the Net.

INTERNET SAFETY TIPS FOR KIDS

1. Before going online, talk with your parents about the rules for safely using the Internet. Set up rules for the time of day and the amount of time you will be allowed on. Discuss what sites you are allowed and not allowed to visit.
2. Never give your real name, address, or phone number out over the Internet. Do not give out any other personal information about your family such as where your parents work or where you go to school.
3. If you find something on the Internet that makes you feel uncomfortable, show your parents right away. Never enter a site that says it is for adults only.
4. Never arrange a meeting with someone you chat or exchange e-mails with unless you have asked your parents first. Make sure you meet in a public place and bring one of your parents along.
5. Do not download any new program without checking with your parents first.
6. Never send your picture or any other family pictures over the Internet to people you have not personally met.

7. If you get a message that makes you feel uncomfortable, do not respond to it. Tell your parents immediately.
8. Never open e-mails with attachments from someone you do not know.
9. Never give out your password to anyone except your parents. Not even your best friend should know your password.
10. Be courteous and polite at all times while on the Internet. Do not do anything that may hurt or scare someone else.

INTERNET ADDICTION

How much is too much? In Germany, some parents concerned about Internet overload are sending their children to a seaside camp where they are allowed only thirty minutes of Internet time a day and regular physical activity is encouraged. In her article "Camp aims to beat web addiction," Tristana Moore reports: "A teenage girl at the camp said: 'My mum always told me to go out and do some sport but I much preferred to play on the computer. It was the only way of not getting bored.'"

For some children, turning to the Internet is a response to social alienation. According to the website Be Web Aware, sponsored by the Media Awareness Network, "Children who are unpopular or shy with peers are often attracted to the opportunities for creating new identities in online communities.... Although playing these games with thousands of other users may appear to be a social activity, for the introverted child or teen, excessive playing can further isolate them from [real-life] friends and peers."

Is your child in danger of Internet addiction? Be concerned if he is unable to leave the computer or craves more Internet time, completely loses track of time while on the Internet, neglects time with family and friends, lets his schoolwork suffer in favor of computer activities, covers up or lies about sites visited or chat room activities. If you feel that your child needs help walking away from the monitor in favor of other activities, you might want to discuss some limits on computer use, find new ways to encourage physical activities and getting together with his peers, or find a way for him to pursue his computer interests in another way (if he's a fan of fantasy games, introduce him to fantasy novels, for a change).

> Media has an incredible ability to replace the family. When kids don't communicate with parents, they will sit and listen to TV, radio, and Walkman. When kids don't feel respected by their parents, the media will accept them for who they are. When parents don't spend time with their kids, the TV is always there to keep them company. And when kids don't feel like we are committed to them, the TV, in search of advertising dollars and rating points, is there to let them know they are important and needed.
>
> —WALT MUELLER, *UNDERSTANDING TODAY'S YOUTH CULTURE*

ADVERTISING AND MARKETING

With a few words on their T-shirts, Abercrombie & Fitch lets young women send a message: "Who needs

a brain when you have these?" A group of female high
school students have a message for A & F: Stop
degrading us.
—JIMMY GREENFIELD, "TEED OFF," *REDEYE MAGAZINE*

Advertising and marketing targeting children teach them
at an early age to want more than they need, and to need
more than they can possibly use. An estimated $15 billion
is spent annually to sell products to children via every
possible media format. Children's marketing has come of
age with increasingly sophisticated ploys to hook kids on
brand-name products. Websites are using a form of
"advergaming" to hook even young children on their
products, from sweetened cereals and drinks to toys. Brand
characters are embedded directly into the entertainment
site's games and activities, and children as young as three
and four are "invited" to log on and play the game. Children
as young as five know that they can order their *Pokemon*,
Digimon, and *Dragonball Z* cards over the Internet. Forget
waiting for Mom or Dad to take them to the store—you
want it, you order it. Preschoolers are considered a "highly
marketable segment for certain products," says a report by
MarketResearch.com. One large retailer lures little ones—
with their parents and their parents' pocketbooks—to its
stores with a marketing scheme called "retailainment."
Toddlers go on "safety scavenger hunts" in the various
departments, following clues and looking for posted safety
tips—and along the way, of course, finding products they
can ask their parents to buy for them.

In her article "Young Eyes on the Prize, Sweepstakes
Increasingly Target Children," Caroline E. Mayer of *The*

Washington Post listed the various prizes that companies dangle in front of children to get them to visit their websites, entice them to buy their product, and to establish brand loyalty. "Barbie is now offering three six- to thirteen-year-old girls a chance to win a shopping spree, makeover, and visit with teen star Lindsay Lohan. And Campbell Soup Co. is touting a chance at a one-week trip to a private island for family and friends—complete with a personal chef to prepare 'favorite kinds of Campbell's soup and SpaghettiOs.' Nickelodeon Television's president, Cyma Zarghami, said, 'If you're a kid, winning stuff is cool…. [Contests] make kids feel important and fulfill their fantasy to make their lives exciting.'"

There is something amiss when a child has to win a contest to "feel important." Is life not exciting enough without a shopping spree or private chef on a private island? One has to wonder why a six-year-old would need a makeover. How does this help a parent trying to give a daughter an opportunity to make her own choices about her looks and her clothing? Does an "expert" need to show her how to look her "best"? If she must look to others (especially an adult or a teen idol) for proper choices about hairstyle and dress at six, she will be a prime candidate for going along with the latest craze—no matter what message comes along with it—when she reaches those all-important teen years.

In his book *Parenting Under Siege*, James Gaborini suggests that advertising and marketing "sow the seeds of later mindless spending and superficial materialism in children that can poison their character development." Advertising and marketing have incredible power to influence peer pressure, which in turn pushes kids to purchase the latest and greatest—hand-me-downs won't do, used is tacky, and cheap is ... well, cheap. Accumulating possessions in order to feel happy and content substitutes material goods for healthy relationships and sabotages a child's desire to share. It becomes all about "me, me, me" and "gimme, gimme, gimme." It is difficult to share generously and to care about the welfare of others when you are busy gathering up goodies for yourself.

Educators are seeing among students of all ages a growing sense of entitlement attached to wealth, and a willingness to taunt and exclude peers based on their economic status. Wealth, the appearance of wealth, and the accumulation of material possessions have become measures of "goodness." If you are poor, there is something wrong with you; you have less value than the wealthier kids. Seven- and eight-year-olds form cliques and exclude those who don't have the necessary status symbols. These cliques become more entrenched in the teen years and can create a poisonous atmosphere in middle schools and high schools. Compounding the problem, school activities have become so expensive that in many places only the elite—i.e., wealthy—in the school can participate. When costs for senior prom skyrocketed in one community, a girl who had spent $2,500 for her prom dress alone commented to a reporter that making prom so expensive "weeded out all those rejects we wouldn't want here anyway."

These twins of commerce—advertising and marketing—also create a false standard of beauty and strength. The bombardment of intense and explicit sexual messages in all forms of media has increased the pressure on girls to become sexualized younger and younger. Couple tha early sexualization with the unrealistic and unattainable airbrushed physical standards of beauty portrayed in the media, and you have a recipe for severe stress, anxiety, and dieting in an attempt to reach unreachable standards. And what is a well-established concern for young girls has become a growing concern for young boys. The airbrushed and bulked-up media "norm" for masculinity has driven young boys to extreme dieting, extreme exercise, and in far too many cases, steroid use in an attempt to reach equally unattainable standards. It is nearly impossible to care deeply for others when you are constantly concerned about your own looks, status, and rank among your peers.

Advertising and marketing also contribute to the message that boys and girls are not equal. Young girls and women are objectified as sexual objects, as come-ons to entice men to buy everything from beer to cars. The intent is to sell product, but young boys are also given the message that girls are not equals to relate to and are instead objects to be used. Creating such a mind-set invites young boys to sexually bully young girls and any boys who do not fit the "norm" for masculinity.

I have discussed the tragedy of sexual bullying in my book *The Bully, The Bullied and the Bystander*. The majority of bullying that goes on in middle school and high school is sexual in nature. Because our sexuality is an integral part of who we are, sexual bullying cuts to the core of our being and can have devastating consequences. Sexual bullying in all its manifestations—verbal, physical, and relational—systematically diminishes a boy's or girl's sense

...ludes sexual rumors or sexual epithets
...ils or lockers, shunning someone because
...er sexual orientation, "scanning" a person's
...aring at breasts, leering, making obscene gestures,
...ogatory terms defining boys as less than "masculine"
(sissy, wuss, pussy, bitch, "you run like a girl"), homophobic
terms (gay, fag, queer, homo), and words used (especially
against girls) to objectify the body, demean sexuality, or
infantilize (fat, dog, "eight," cunt, pussy, lez, slut, whore,
hooker, babe, baby, chick, kitten). Bullying can also
include threats to sexually violate the target, verbal assess-
ments of the target's body, sexist or sexual jokes, or
derogatory comments about sexual performance or lack of
sexual activity. Add to all of these the displaying or circu-
lating of sexually explicit material intended to shame or
humiliate or degrade, the wearing of clothes or pins that
have sexually offensive sayings or pictures, or the existence
of sexually explicit graffiti, and you have the ingredients
for creating what the Canadian Human Rights Commission (1991) and the United States Civil Rights Act of 1964
have identified as a hostile environment that interferes
with a student's ability to learn. Compound all of that with
music lyrics, music videos, and sexual and sexist cyber-
bullying, and the moral climate that kids are experiencing
daily can be rank.

After the president of Harvard University, Lawrence
Summers, suggested that women might be inherently
inferior to men in math and science, Rushworth M. Kidder,
author and founder of Global Ethics, noted that the public
response was "instant and galvanic." President Summers
(who later apologized) was "battered by sternly worded

statements insisting on the fundamental equality of the sexes." But while riding a double-decker bus up London's Regent Street, Kidder could not help but notice the apparent disconnect between the celebration of equality and freedoms for women—they could earn their own money and spend it as they wished, could walk around freely in the square as their great-grandmothers could not have done without a male relative—and the scantily clad, provocatively posed mannequins behind the plate-glass windows. He wrote in the *Global Ethics Newsletter:*

> The windows fairly throb with the mind-numbing demand: You must dress for sex, think of yourself in sexual terms, and use every opportunity to promote sex.... [W]omen are essentially objects of allure. As such they are absolutely dependent on men, without whom their highest objective goes unfulfilled. What if, as Harvard Yard argues, women are fully equal to men of professional acumen and academic prowess. Regent Street couldn't care less. That equality, it would say, is either irrelevant to a woman's destiny or strictly subservient to her true hormonal goals.... So powerful is the message of woman as sexual icon— driven home through movies, music, television, magazines, and every other avenue of pop culture— that the manipulation has become strangely invisible. Where is the voice of outrage ...?

Kidder suggests that the moral outrage of Harvard Yard needs to be brought to the demeaning allure of Regent

Street. Traditional biases and conventional stereotypes cannot be rejected and high moral and intellectual parity accepted so long as we continue to accept the fashionable debasing of women's identity in media.

It is not just advertising that debases. Media entertainment encourages the denigration and subjugation of girls and women. Violence combined with sex is seen as fun, and as sport. Sports, violence, fun, and sex were combined at a Super Bowl game (as if they weren't there already) to create what is now referred to as the "Janet Jackson Incident." During the half-time "entertainment" Justin Timberlake ripped Janet Jackson's costume to briefly expose her breast. The howls of disgust at such "obscenity" were loud and numerous. Complaints poured in to the network and to the FCC. One parent sued the network for the psychological damage done to her family, who were subjected to a nipple exposed at a "family-friendly" football game. Congressional hearings were held. Large fines were levied.

Whether it was an intentional or unintentional part of the act, and whether Janet Jackson was a willing or unwilling participant, were issues left unexplored by the media. But a more glaring lapse was the failure on the part of commentators, news reporters, columnists, religious leaders, and the public in general to register any complaints about the role played by Justin Timberlake. His actions, which amounted to simulated sexual violence against a woman (i.e., ripping her clothes to expose her breast), were denounced by very few people, and those who dared to raise their voices were themselves denounced or ridiculed. Has such sexual violence become so commonplace that it does not even register as a violent act in the consciousness of spectators? Where is the outrage?

Perhaps as a society we are numb. After such a steady diet of violence, gender bias, exploitation, and sport we are desensitized to, but not immune from, the message of media.

AGES AND STAGES

Critical engagement means to be aware of our media world, to reflect on it, to inquire about the world views and values it presents, the techniques used to construct it and why. Media literacy—that is, critical engagement with our media culture—is about inquiry and helping us live mindfully.

—SISTER ROSE PACATTE, "TV'S NOT A BLACK
AND WHITE ISSUE," U.S. CATHOLIC

The media is not going away, and it will only become more intertwined in our children's lives in the future. Forbidding them to interact with the media that surrounds them will be futile. Taking a sledgehammer to the TV, hiding the headphones, banning the DVDs, and unplugging the computer is no guarantee that media will not influence our children. Kids need to be guided by us through instructional experiences that enhance their moral awareness, strengthen their sense of moral responsibility, and refine their ability to process what they see with a more critical eye. That means we need to be aware of the messages our children are being asked to understand, interpret, and assimilate daily. It is also important to understand children's developmental levels and their own tolerance for media content.

PRESCHOOLERS

Preschoolers like action and surprise and try to make meaning out of what they are seeing. To them Simba is real, and the sadness he feels at the death of his father is one a preschooler feels as well. A preschooler who insists on viewing *The Lion King* again and again might run out of the room before the scary stuff and begin anticipating the sad parts in advance of the scenes. As long as your preschooler's favorite scary characters are not making him fearful or keeping him awake at night, join in the fun. Pay attention to themes that could threaten his sense of security and well-being. Avoid any shows that depict realistic scenes of violence. Aggressive behavior should be imaginary and unrealistic in nature.

Children at this age have trouble separating pretend and make-believe from real. Be aware and beware of movies and cartoons made for older children and adults. Four-year-olds might love dinosaurs, but the reality of *Jurassic Park* doesn't match with their images of these wonderful beasts they love to hold in their hands. Young children who watch the news can't yet understand that it is not a running commentary of all that has happened in the day but is merely a condensed version with most of the good stuff left out and the bad stuff magnified. With the ugly and hurtful magnified, some young children—especially bright, imaginative ones—can become overwhelmed by their own fantasies. This should be a sign to you that more real play and less TV is in order for this child.

SIX- TO TWELVE-YEAR-OLDS

The various media tools and the messages they convey fascinate six- to twelve-year-olds. They can follow plots and not only anticipate but try to predict what will happen next. However, children under nine cannot effectively separate fantasy from reality in shows and in advertisements—and they often have a hard time distinguishing entertainment from ads.

Harry Potter movies and books follow a plot, create fantasy, mix reality with that fantasy, and contain all kinds of lessons about relationships and how the world operates. *Jurassic Park* does the same. The line between what is real and what is not real is thin at this age, and this will affect a child's response to violence on the screen. If there is violence in the show, is it gratuitous, or does it make sense within the context of theme, storyline, and character development? Does it minimize or gloss over the real effects and consequences of the violence, or does it portray violence and its outcomes realistically? Scary can be fun and thrilling or it can be just plain scary. In J. K. Rowling's *Harry Potter and the Prisoner of Azkaban*, the young wizard is tormented by a convict hunting for him, by omens foreshadowing his death, and by prison guards who seem to have strange powers over him. It is darker and scarier than the previous *Harry Potter* movies, and younger children who found the earlier movies exciting, a bit scary, and fun might find this one frightening. Older kids might enjoy the fright and take away from the movie the message of perseverance and resilience.

Kids at this age venture outside of the home alone and over to friends' homes, where they might be exposed to adult-oriented programing. If kids are comfortable telling you about the good, the bad, and the ugly in their daily lives, without being ridiculed, interrogated, or punished, they are more likely to be open with you about their media experiences.

Between six and nine, kids are interested in the facts—not long-drawn-out explanations. They usually have little interest in members of the opposite sex, but are very interested in learning about their own bodies—and visiting the websites that show the body dissected and sliced to reveal the muscles, nerves, and skeletal structure. You're enjoying the amazing graphics; they're enjoying the blood and gore.

Between nine and eleven it is time to capitalize on your preteens' interest as it grows beyond their own bodies to include their minds and emotions. The media are presenting them with a lot of mixed messages about sexuality, sex, love, dating, diseases, and pimples—and they are starting to pay attention. Now is the time they need to know the detailed facts about sexuality, intimacy, dating, and sexually transmitted diseases. The more knowledge they have from you as a reliable source, the better equipped they will be to bring the misinformation and distortions they see and hear in the media and bounce them off the accurate and honest information they got from you. If your information is scanty, and for many of us it is, you can scour libraries, bookstores, video stores, and the Internet for books and media that not only impart accurate information but also present it in a way that mirrors the values you want to share with your children. You will no doubt find others that don't. Some of them can be used as jumping-off points to discuss with your children why the information they impart might be suspect.

If you listen and watch with your preteens, you will be able to guide them to making good media and music choices in much the same way you guide them in all other areas of their life—by increasingly giving them opportunities to make their own choices and decisions, while simultaneously decreasing limits and boundaries. Sandwiched in between these two is your own willingness to listen to your children and your courage to take a stand when it is absolutely necessary for your child's safety and well-being. There are times to say no, to mean it, and to follow through with it.

It is at this age that kids also take an interest in the bigger world outside their own neighborhood. In his bestseller *Familyhood: Nurturing the Values that Matter*, Dr. Lee Salk suggests watching news shows together with your older children, and being available to react and to talk to them about the subject matter:

> Programs that deal with painful topics or news stories about war or natural disasters can help sensitize children to human suffering and make them aware of the greater world and historical events. They can be helped to understand about the very real ravages of war and the fact that injustice and great cruelty occur.... Talk about your own dismay that such things can happen. Make it clear that you are moved and deeply concerned about what you see and that everyone must do what he or she can do to prevent bad things from happening in the world.

Teaching children at this age to be media savvy also involves watching commercials with them and teaching them to find the lies, deceptions, half-truths, quick fixes, lures, and bias. They will have a difficult time making intelligent, thoughtful purchase decisions before the age of twelve. Advertisements and marketing aimed specifically at children can subtly undermine your family's values of living simply, sharing generously, and helping willingly by enticing your children to spend recklessly and consume more and more goods in order to live the "good life." By example and through dialogue you can help your kids understand Maurice Sendak's line: "There must be more to life than having everything."

TEENAGERS

Teenagers are moving toward independence in all areas of their lives. No longer seeing you as their parent, they look to you as a mentor and a guide when it comes to issues such as responsible and respectful behavior. They will increasingly assume more and more responsibility for their own physical, intellectual, moral, and sexual growth.

Able to discern deeper meaning in emotional expressions—a laugh may indeed be masking nervousness or sadness—they gravitate toward television shows, music, and video that express a wide range of feelings, and combinations of conflicting feelings.

If you want to stay in touch with what is going on in your teenagers' lives, you will need to balance your involvement and your necessary distance as a caring adult. That means making your home the place kids like to come to. It's your television they are watching, your computer they are logged on to, and the music they are listening to, the conversations they are having are within your earshot. And when you are alone with your own teenagers, take time to just be there to watch a movie they want to watch, or listen to their music with them. Ask them to teach you some "web language" and show you some streets and alleyways on the Net. When you are willing to be in their world without being so quick to judge or to ridicule, they are more willing to let you in and be open to your guidance.

Their interest in the global neighborhood expands from one of mere curiosity to wanting to become more involved. This involvement can drive parents crazy if it leads to chatting online with peers all over the world at odd hours of the night. Teenagers suffering from speech anomalies or who are extremely shy often open up in the world of cyber-socializing. Kids will say things online that they would never say face to face. That can be good, in the sense of helping kids to improve their communication skills; and that can be bad, as it might expose them to bad language, put-downs, ugly rumors, and death threats.

Your teenager might take a political stand contrary to your own, because he is doing research on the Internet about information that was omitted from his political science textbook. The challenging debate that follows will help you determine if this is reputable information—and just new to you—or information acquired from a website with a negative or misleading agenda.

Teenagers begin to assert their own personal values as their own, not cookie-cutter versions of yours. They will quickly take you to task over any discrepancy in your professed values and your lived ones ("Mom, you swore at that kid," "Dad you didn't take your hat off when we visited Grandma"). This provides you with an opportunity to help them use that same ability to discern discrepancy in the media's mixed messages: "Are they really interested in your happiness or just in separating you from your money?" "Why do you suppose they chose that woman to play that role? That man?" "Did the music they selected for that scene change the emotional message of the script?" "Was that truly funny or did the laugh track prod you into laughing at someone else's pain?"

DEADENING CONSEQUENCES—WHAT'S SO WRONG WITH ALL THIS VIOLENCE?

The best and deepest moral training is that which one gets by having to enter into proper relations with others.

—JOHN DEWEY

Everything a child is exposed to—whether real, viewed, listened to, or imagined—becomes a part of that child's view of the world. Real or imagined acts of violence tend to cultivate a sense of danger, mistrust, alienation, and gloom. Children who are regularly exposed to media violence are apt to become *desensitized* to real-life violence. As a consequence, they are less likely to be sensitive to the pain and suffering of others and thus less likely to respond to someone in need or to help out in a crisis. They are more likely to be numb, apathetic, and callous when they become aware of or see a peer being harmed. They are more willing to tolerate ever-increasing levels of violence in their everyday world. They become habituated to a violent, crude, and rude society, taking it for granted and unable to visualize a life that is different.

Kids *imitate* the violence they see and hear. There is a clear correlation between exposure to violence and the development and display of aggressive values and behavior. Kids who habitually watch media violence tend to behave more aggressively and use aggression to try to solve problems. In an extensive quantitative review of literature concerning television, researchers George Comstock and Haejung Paik concluded, "The strongest association between exposure to television violence and antisocial and aggressive behavior is the amount of exposure both to television violence *and* to aggressive and antisocial behavior." If children are exposed to violence—including physical punishment—in their homes *and* watch media violence, they are more likely than their peers to display aggressive behavior toward those peers. Recent research has demonstrated that children who are bullied by peers or older siblings *and* repeatedly exposed to media violence—often as an escape from their own reality—are far more likely than their peers to resort to violence to solve their own relationship problems with others.

Kids who are regularly exposed to media violence are apt to become easily *intimidated*. Sustained intimidation can lead to depression. The amount of violence depicted in media far outstrips the actual violence committed in real-world communities. Kids who become saturated with media violence come to believe that the world is an unsafe and violent place. They become fearful and distrustful of others, overreacting to slights and minor incidents. They begin to view anyone outside of their immediate circle of acquaintance as a threat to their safety and well-being. Since they are fearful most of the time, they tend to miss their natural, healthy fear clues when something is terribly wrong. They are lulled into thinking that they are safe when in familiar surroundings with familiar people.

WHAT CAN YOU DO?

> Like the force of nature, the digital age cannot be denied or stopped. It has four very powerful qualities that will result in ultimate triumph: decentralizing, globalizing, harmonizing, and empowering.
> —NICHOLAS NEGROPONTE, *BEING DIGITAL*

1. Move the television, computer, and DVD player into a public area of your home.
2. Listen to what your children are listening to and talk with them about the message in relation to your values and expectations.
3. Play an active role in selecting material that is suitable for your younger children, and teach older children to make healthy choices about their media consumption and interaction.
4. Watch TV shows and movies with your children and talk with them about plot, characters, themes, intentions, and manipulative tools.

5. Encourage your children to take you on a tour of their Internet communities, and discuss together what you find there.

6. Look at advertising in all the media forms with your kids and help them learn to decipher the message and to be discerning consumers.

7. Form a movie club (like a book club) with other families and select, watch, and discuss the movies together. Do these shows teach values you would like your children to learn?

8. Be alert to the four danger signs of overexposure to "uncivilizing" media: desensitization to violence, numbing, imitation, and intimidation.

9. Teach your children basic Net etiquette and Net safety.

10. Encourage kids to get involved with their peers in activities that promote creative, responsible, prosocial, and civil behaviors.

11. Stay involved with your children—unplug the television, turn off the computer, confiscate the batteries to the Game Boy, and lose the headphones. Get outside and explore your own neighborhood together, get involved in a community project, cruise a river, climb a rock wall, ride bikes, take a hike, share a picnic lunch, look at the stars. It's a big galaxy out there.

Children who mature in a secure home with parents who explore all of the dimensions of humanity in a non-hurried, accepting atmosphere can probably handle most electronic media without damaging their dual memory and response systems. They'll tend to delay their responses, to look deeper than the surface of things. Further, they'll probably prefer to spend more time in direct interaction with real people. They will thus develop the sense of balance that permits them to be part of the real and electronic worlds—but also to stand apart from them.

—DR. ROBERT SYLVESTER

Chapter 5

Hoarding, Harming:
Betraying Ourselves and
Our Circle of Caring

If only there were evil people somewhere, insidiously committing evil deeds, and it were necessary only to separate them from the rest of us and destroy them. But the line dividing good and evil cuts through the heart of every human being. And who is willing to destroy a piece of his own heart?"
—ALEXANDER SOLZHENITSYN, *THE GULAG ARCHIPELAGO*

Hating, hoarding, and harming are the three virulent agents that can rip apart the fabric of human relationships. They destroy our sense of community, our solidarity with one another, and our self-respect. The "I and Thou" and "We" are rendered null and void.

Hate is by far the most virulent of the three agents; it is evil in action. In *Becoming Evil: How Ordinary People Commit Genocide and Mass Killing*, James Waller defines human evil as "the deliberate harming of humans by other humans." It is the destructive things we do to each other. He contends that "our awareness of our own capacity for evil—and ways to cultivate the moral sensibilities that curb that capacity— is the best safeguard we can have against future genocides and mass killings." Hating is the way we give expression and form to our capacity for evil. That capacity can be curbed only by loving-kindness and compassion. It is impossible to care deeply about someone and simultaneously hate them— be upset, angry, disappointed, frustrated, yes—but not hate. The subject of hate—and what can be done to counteract it—will be discussed in the next chapter.

Hoarding and harming do cause hurt, but they are not necessarily acts of cruelty or evil in and of themselves. However, the consequences of hoarding and harming can be both mean and cruel. And both hoarding and harming can be called into the service of hate to further evil. Most importantly, hoarding and harming create cracks in our solidarity with one another.

The moral sensibilities that can curb hoarding and harming are *sharing generously* and *helping willingly*. As we reach out to share generously, it is difficult to be greedy, avaricious, covetous, and stingy. And helping others implies that we are not causing hurt, injury, or unnecessary suffering.

Teaching our children to think and act ethically is threefold. It is giving them ways to care deeply, share generously, and help willingly; curb their inclinations to hoard or harm; and stop in its tracks anything that fuels hatred. We know in our heads all of this to be true, but as the moral theologian Hans Küng explained, "yet to be lived in heart and action."

HOARD

If appetite is a gift, and greed a sin, then waste is a
crime. We waste our food, our energy, our time, our
lives. We seek power from the accumulation of
surplus; we are greedy for more than our fair share. In
a finite world, we search for infinite satiation…. Our
planet groans under the burden of this greed.
— B. K. S. IYENGAR, *LIGHT ON LIFE, THE YOGA JOURNEY*
TO WHOLENESS, INNER PEACE, AND ULTIMATE FREEDOM

Hoarding is about me, mine, and more—to the detriment of
us, ours, and enough. We are eating more, accumulating
more, and wanting more. Trips to the mall replace trips to
the park. Elaborate gifts replace time spent together. Status
symbols replace functional wares. We lock ourselves inside
our houses and gate others out. We try to "keep up with the
Joneses," to have the biggest, the boldest, and the best. Our
children are watching and learning.

Susie insists on three different, elaborate costumes for
the three different activities she will take part in on
Hallowe'en—the class party, her soccer team's after-school
event, and her trip around the neighborhood for treats.
Samuel hopes to wow judges and take the top prize again
this year with three costumes in the same contest. One
costume is no longer enough for the fantasy of the holiday.
Homemade costumes are frowned upon. Kids are pitted
against one another for top prizes. One company sells
children's costumes studded with Swarovski crystals that
range in price from $400 to $1,600. Adults accompany
their children trick-or-treating dressed themselves in $1,000

Darth Vader outfits. Greed, waste, and power are all wrapped up in one day's activities for children. Gone is the imagination, the fun, the sharing, and the creativity—and forget collecting money for UNICEF. As one costume-maker said, "It gets competitive out there on the playground."

This competition to have the first, the best, and the most is a potent source of the divisiveness that can wreak havoc with our sense of community. The disparity between the haves and the have-nots grows bigger, and with it the dangerous us-them dichotomy that seriously impedes the development of children's capacity to care deeply about others. Instead, children look down on those with less, and envy those with more.

Children's play and adult technology are merging as three-year-olds have their own DVD players, four-year-olds sport their own Tuff Stuff computers, six-year-olds are being sold their own LeapFrog cellphones, eight-year-olds are grabbing up digital cameras and printers; ten-year-olds are plugged into their color-coded iPods and tuned out to the world around them. No longer are the toys make-believe computers, phones, or cameras. They are the real thing, and real toys are left in the toybox in favor of solo electronic activities that don't merely mimic adult activities, they replicate them.

Becoming more isolated, self-centered, and competitive as they accumulate more gadgets around them, children are losing opportunities to care and share, solve problems collaboratively, and simply play together—so critical for developing important social skills and a sense of solidarity with one another. When they are greedy, they are never contented, never satisfied, and always afraid there will not be enough. Yoga teacher B. K. S. Iyengar called such children "rich beggars," always wanting more.

> My life continues to be enriched by connecting with everyday humanity. Each time I do this, I rediscover that what I have been given is far beyond monetary value. And I reaffirm that everyone is worthy—and worth knowing.
>
> —MARJORIE HAMLIN, "I'VE BEEN ENRICHED BY BEGGARS," *THE CHRISTIAN SCIENCE MONITOR*

HARM—THE BETRAYAL OF TRUST

> The shortest and surest way to live with honor in the world is to be in reality what we would appear to be; all human virtues increase and strengthen themselves by the practice and experience of them.
>
> —SOCRATES

Being trusting and trustworthy enables us to create friendships and other kinds of caring relationships, as well as enter into contracts and make commitments. Trust is the social thread that ties each of us, one to another, and together as a whole community. When there is no trust, two people dance solitary dances around one another—each in their own world—neither daring to be open and vulnerable to the other. When a trust is betrayed, the ties that bind us together are tattered or severed.

Disagreements and conflicts happen *within* the bonds of relationships. They are normal, natural, and necessary. Our job as wise and caring parents is to teach our children how to handle those conflicts peacefully and nonviolently ("You may both turn the TV on when you have a plan you both can live with"). Within the powerful bonds of friendships, children get ample opportunity to practice resolving conflicts and treating one another kindly, fairly, and justly. Lying, cheating, and stealing can *rip apart* those bonds. The reasons not to lie, cheat, or steal are to keep one's own integrity (the I), to maintain and strengthen the bond with another (the Thou), and to live in a peaceful and just community.

Lying, cheating, and stealing are truth and honesty's hollow impostors cloaked in any number of disguises: deception, half-truths, and the absence of truth. There are any number of ways that trust can be betrayed. We can tell the truth technically and be lying if that truth is only half of the truth. It is possible to deceive without saying a word, to violate a trust with a truth told that breaks a promise. To cheat by lying or cheat by stealing another student's project proposal. Steal someone else's coat or steal someone else's boyfriend. Destroy someone's reputation with an ugly rumor or decimate someone's sense of self with relentless taunting.

By far the most serious offences against truth are those that are intended to hurt someone. In his *Pensées*, Blaise Pascal wrote, "The abuse of truth ought to be as much punished as the introduction of a falsehood. As if there were two hells, one for sins against love, the other for sins against justice."

The more children anchor their actions in deep caring for themselves and for others, the less likely they will be to succumb to the lure of these three thieves that rob them of their own integrity and of their relationships with others.

Individualism, with its rapacious and exploitive attitude toward the world, is the antithesis of that individuality which is the authentic self realized within the genuine community.

—PAGE SMITH

LYING

Lying is done with words and also with silence.

—ADRIENNE RICH

Hindu sage Sai Baba taught his students, "Before you speak, ask yourself, is it kind, is it necessary, is it true, does it improve on the silence?" Far more than teaching children merely not to lie, we need to teach them to be kind with their words, truthful and trustworthy. It is important that people can count on them to be honest and true to their word. Lies are the absence of truth, and they wear many guises: spoken, bald-faced lies ("I didn't do it"), acts of commission ("I did too brush my teeth," "We were just teasing her—we didn't really mean to make her cry"), acts of omission ("Don't tell her where we've been—just let her think we went to school"), or deception ("I was at Sue's house all night").

In his book *On Bullshit*, moral philosopher Harry Frankfurt wrote about something even more hollow and dangerous than outright lies. "The liar knows what the truth is and he is concerned with trying to keep people away from the truth. [This] shows a respect for the truth and the value of truth. Whereas the bullshitter does not care at all.... The liar is limited by his commitment to saying something that conflicts with the truth ... the bullshitter who doesn't care about the truth can go where he likes." When one has absolute contempt for veracity, doctoring data to match the desired outcome can have serious consequences for the target of the doctored data. Targets of bullies rack their brains trying to figure out what on earth they ever did to ask for the horrific verbal, physical, or relational attack to which they are being subjected. The reality is that they did nothing to deserve such contempt. The bully fabricated it all to isolate the targeted child, who then becomes a loner and a loser—and nobody wants to hang with a loser.

This kind of fabrication has nothing to do with a different kind of lie—the lie that is inherent in the wonderful world of fiction that fascinates young and old alike. Salman Rushdie called fiction "the great lie that tells the truth about life." Picasso called art "the lie that makes us realize the truth."

Fairy tales hold such a fascination with small children because up until age five or six there is a blurring of distinction between reality and fantasy. Mr. Rogers's neighbors are real, and Cookie Monster really does love cookies, and there really are monsters under the bed, and Simba's father really did die. And yes, the imaginary friend, Simone, really did eat that cookie that is missing from the cookie jar. Fantasies that invite "suspension of disbelief" help children develop their creativity, imagination, and agency—I am powerful and capable! This suspension of disbelief will enable them, as they grow older, to enjoy and learn from fiction. Children who enjoy make-believe will also be able to imagine creative solutions to difficult problems.

Children at this age who are not punished but rather are disciplined, listened to, and cared for are less likely to resort to lying to cover up what they have done. If a child has the remnants of a cookie on her face, asking her in a stern voice, "Did you eat that cookie?" invites a lie in order to avoid the punishment that is sure to follow that question, no matter the answer. Making a comment—"Looks like a luscious chocolate chip cookie on your face. That will be your dessert eaten early. Let's talk." "I found a dinosaur in your jacket when I was getting ready to wash it. We need to make sure it gets back to its owner"—is more likely to produce a dialogue, a display of healthy guilt if warranted, and a way to move on. You are more likely to get the truth when you don't demand it or make threats but talk about the reality that you see or know.

School-age children are dishonest in order to avoid doing something, to deny responsibility for mischief, or to cover up another deception. Just as Pinocchio's nose grew as he told more and more lies, your children will feel some discomfort, and it will usually show up in their facial expressions and uncomfortable body movements. It is important that they not get away with their lies, as they can easily fall into a pattern of lying just because they can. If you punish them for their lies, they will probably bring their deceptions further underground and learn to put on a "poker face." If they continue to get away with their lies without any consequences, as they enter the teen years they will not likely feel any internal conflict or guilt about lying.

The more your children can share the good, the bad, and the ugly without fear of punishment, the less likely they'll feel a need to lie. And if they do lie, they know they will need to own it, fix it, and learn from it.

Just being caught is a relief for some kids so that a bigger problem can be addressed. Very small for his age, Jonathan was skipping his gym class because other boys were tormenting him in the locker room. Jonathan made up elaborate stories about what fun he was having in the gym. When his dad calmly told him that the teacher called to report the absences and asked Jonathan to "talk to me about it," Jonathan broke down crying and told his dad what the other boys had done to him. If he had feared punishment, he might have merely taken the punishment for the lie, given a lame excuse for his absences, and stuffed all of his pain inside.

Since this is the time when strong friendships are developing beyond the playmate stage of early childhood, we need to talk with children about the importance of being a good and trustworthy friend—and how a lie, deception, or half-truth can tear apart a friendship. The way we interact at home influences the way our children develop the social skills that help them to make and keep friends. Every opportunity your child has to care, share, and help around the house will make it more likely that she will do the same in her friendships outside the home.

Teenagers, moving into what Dr. Ron Taffel calls the "second family" of peers, feel confident that they can "live and lie behind an almost seamless wall of silence," and in essence lock parents out of their real lives. Your son can have a serious drinking problem and you are totally oblivious to it, but when he ends up in the hospital with alcohol poisoning, the whispers from his peers confirmed that they all knew. When your daughter finally can't hide her bulimia from you, her friends openly talk about where and when she regularly purged her lunch.

In his book *Breaking through to Teens*, Dr. Taffel wrote that when he got to know these kids he discovered "they still need what young people have always needed: nurture, appreciation, clarity in expectations, and a sense of belonging." The tragedy of our times is that most adolescents do not get these basic needs met by adults and do not feel truly "at home" within their own families. And it is to this second family that they migrate to find what is missing in their lives. The more kids omit critical details about their life or fabricate to cover them up, the further they slip away from their first family into this second family—and the more high-risk behaviors become "normal behaviors."

The skepticism you nurtured in them when they were three is the same friendly skepticism you will want to have now. Is he really spending the night at his friend's house? Will the parents be home—and do you even know these parents enough to make a friendly call and offer to provide some snacks for the movie night that is happening at their house? And if your daughter does sneak out the window after you've locked the front door, you'll have a better crack at dealing with the issue effectively if you don't ground her for six months, but put the onus on her to figure out how she can regain your trust, because you do want to trust her again. And yes, you will let the school secretary know your son will not be in school today, but you will not lie for him. And yes, you will tell your daughter's classmate that your daughter can't come to the phone right now and that she will return the call shortly, but no, you will not say that she is not here.

Once again, how you behave matters. You pay full ticket price for your son, even though he could pass for eleven years old. You don't lie to your mother-in-law about why you can't come for dinner this weekend. You don't fabricate a story about why your son is dropping out of hockey. You keep your word when you have promised to take your daughter to her friend's house.

The Good Lie:

Good lies are told in the service of a greater good. They are a last resort when there is no truthful alternative. If in Bosnia you are hiding a Muslim under the floorboards in your living room and Milosovic's henchmen come knocking, you lie. If a child is home alone and a stranger calls asking for his parents, you hope he will lie. Teaching children that such lies are sometimes necessary for a greater good—not an excuse or an easy way out—will help them begin to develop the necessary tools to begin working through moral dilemmas. The good lie is not in and of itself a moral dilemma. To tell the truth about his parents' not being home is to put the young boy at risk of serious personal harm. In fact, in the service of deep caring, no decent choice other than the lie readily presents itself. The first scenario presents a more difficult choice. The dilemma presented itself one step back, when you made the decision to hide the young woman. Knowing you could be killed along with her if she were discovered, you made a moral choice. A moral dilemma arises when two virtues clash and no easy resolution presents itself. It can't be resolved by pretending that one virtue is right and the other is wrong. Medical advances have presented all of us with ethical choices and moral dilemmas unheard of even a few years ago. Our children will be faced with choices as difficult and even more complex than the ones we are faced with today.

A neuroscientist at Princeton University, Joshua Greene, used brain scans to map how human brains make sense of moral dilemmas. He found out that sometimes the various parts of the brain work together, sometimes they compete with one another, "and that's what makes a moral decision difficult, when there are different kinds of processes in the brain that are sort of duking it out." On the difficult personal dilemmas, in all of the volunteers there was initially spiked brain activity in the region known to regulate emotions, followed by spiked brain activity in the part of the brain that is known to signal conflict. Depending on which way the volunteer chose to resolve the dilemma, two other different parts of the brain became more active.

One of the dilemmas was a scenario in which you and your baby are hiding with a group of people and your baby's cry threatens to give you all away. Would you be willing to smother the baby in order to save the rest of the group?

One piece of information that Greene came up with that fascinated me was that those who said they would sacrifice the baby to save the others had spiked activity in the part of the brain associated with cognitive activity (cost-benefit analysis). Those who chose not to smother the baby had increased activity in the area of the brain that signals "emotional intuition." This appears to be an ethic rooted in deep caring.

Today I bent the truth to be kind, and I have no regret, for I am far surer of what is kind than I am of what is true.

—ROBERT BRAULT

CHEATING

To cheat and to lie is to be alone.
—ROBERT COLES, *THE MORAL INTELLIGENCE OF CHILDREN*

A seven-year-old moves her game piece two spaces when her friend is not looking. A ten-year-old sells his completed homework to classmates for five dollars per assignment. A twelve-year-old uses his brother's ski pass and lends his brother his movie pass. A thirteen-year-old writes the answers to an exam on the brim of her hat. A sixteen-year-old buys his term paper off the Internet. A seventeen-year-old "throws" a baseball game.

Commenting on a nationwide survey by the Center for Academic Integrity on cheating in high school, the Rutgers University professor who conducted the survey, Donald McCabe, said one of the most common reasons students gave for cheating was that the adult world sets such a poor example. "I think kids today are looking to adults and society for a moral compass, and when they see the behavior occurring there, they don't understand why they should be held to a higher standard."

One student elaborated, "What's important is getting ahead. The better the grades you have, the better school you get into, the better you are going to do in life. And if you learn to cut corners to do that, you're going to be saving yourself time and energy. In the real world, that's what's going to be going on. The better you do, that's what shows. It's not how moral you were getting there."

Choosing *looking good* over *doing good*: obviously this student had never heard of a schoolteacher, Christine Pelton, or a golfer, Babe Didrikson Zaharias.

Downloading Science Projects:

Caught plagiarizing their science projects, twenty-eight high school sophomores in Christine Pelton's biology class received no credit for their work and therefore would fail the class. Parents went to the Piper District School Board protesting that the failing grades were unfair. Some thought the kids plagiarized unintentionally; others complained that the teacher did not explain to her students exactly what plagiarism was; others said their children had downloaded only parts of the project.

The school board caved and told Ms. Pelton that the students should be given partial credit, so that most would pass the class. Ms. Pelton refused to change the grades and resigned from her teaching position rather than "punish those students who had turned in original science projects."

The *Kansas City Star* newspaper received a few letters of support for the board and many more letters of support for the teacher who refused to give in. One letter to the editor, from James S. Walker, former president of Jamestown College, summed up the issue: "As a retired college president, I would ask the school board this question: 'When you have sacrificed academic integrity, what's left? Plagiarism is stealing. Would the school board have condoned the theft of physical property as well as intellectual property?'"

It was easier for the parents to rescue their teenagers from the consequences of their theft of intellectual property and blame the teacher than to hold their sons and daughters accountable. Theft 1, Integrity 0.

A Golf Ball and a Choice:

A noted authority on responsibility-oriented education and peaceful conflict resolution, Constance Dembrowsky writes in her curriculum program for teenagers, *Mastering Anger* (www.iasd.com), the story of the famed professional golfer Babe Didrikson Zaharias. In a tournament in which she was strokes ahead of her peers

with only a few holes remaining, her first shot off the tee went wide and landed in the rough. She found the ball in the rough, and hit a fabulous shot that landed on the green. If she could make the putt, she would be another stroke under par, putting her in a better position to win. As she got ready to putt the ball, she realized from the markings on it that the ball was not the brand she used. The ball she hit out of the rough was not hers. She never took that shot. She reported the error, a violation of the rules, to the officials and disqualified herself from the tournament.

"Why did you do that? You had a great chance to win the tournament. Nobody would have ever known," a friend said to her later in the clubhouse.

Babe replied, "But I would have known."

The lesson goes on to talk with teens about making such a difficult—some would say foolish—choice. If the way you get something (a golf trophy, a science grade) does not maintain dignity and respect for yourself and others, then you have sacrificed your integrity, your honor, and your self-respect. The cost is high. If you can't get it in a way that maintains respect for yourself and others, it's not worth having.

Babe Didrikson Zaharias walked away that day with something a stolen tournament win could not give her—her integrity. Christine Pelton stood up for those who did not cheat, and walked away from a teaching job rather than violate her integrity.

When asked about companies such as turnitin.com that check students' papers for signs of plagiarism, Professor McCabe recommended what Constance was advocating for her students, what Christine Pelton quit her job over, and what Babe Didrikson Zaharias forfeited a title for: "I subscribe to the theory that suggests we'd be much better off promoting integrity among our students rather than trying to police their dishonesty."

> Trust and integrity are precious resources, easily squandered, hard to regain. They can thrive only on a foundation for respect for veracity.
> —SISSELA BOK, *LYING: MORAL CHOICE IN PUBLIC AND PRIVATE LIFE*

STEALING

> My real life lesson came when attempting to define the difference between truth and honesty. What I finally realized is that my truth is not another person's truth, while what is honest is a fact that remains the same thing to both of us no matter what our differences might be in morality, ethics, and integrity.
> —DIANNE S. REEVES

A two-year-old understands very clearly what is "mine." What she doesn't yet understand is that not everything she wants is hers. It isn't until three or four that a child begins to understand that some things are "mine," some things are "yours," and some things "belong to all of us" to be shared. It is not uncommon for a three-year-old to "borrow a toy" from the preschool toybox to play with at home because it interested her and she didn't want to give it up yet.

Making sure your child has a few special toys that he does not need to share with a younger brother or a playmate, other toys that he needs to share, and others that belong to everyone in the family will help him begin to understand the difference between personal property and communal property, as well as give him opportunities to share willingly.

The sooner your children get an allowance the sooner they will be able to learn to spend, save, and give to those who have less than they do. Having their own money can help them be more selective about what items they decide they really want, and help teach them to handle their money in a way that will serve them well now as preschoolers, and later when they have a paper route or babysit, and in the teen years when they have a summer or part-time job.

Elementary-age children need to learn how to ask for what they need and want in a kind way ("May I take this toy home tonight? I will bring it back tomorrow"). But knowing proper borrowing manners doesn't mean your child won't steal something from the store or from a friend's home. Children steal for many reasons, the least of which is because they *need* it. They may do it on a dare, to impress their friends with gifts, to punish, or to fill up a hole in their heart—accumulating goods to make up for feeling lonely or angry.

They may be taking money out of your purse because they want to buy extra snacks at school but know you will say no if they ask for the money. They may be stealing money out of your wallet because another child is extorting it from them. Your son figures it is far better to have dad mad than have the older kids beat him up because he didn't show up with the money.

Teens steal for these same reasons, plus other reasons and excuses ("Hey, it's a big corporation, they won't miss it," "Everybody does it," "I've got to impress my girl-friend"). If the stealing is a regular occurrence, or is a part of a bigger behavioral issue—drug or alcohol abuse or other destructive behaviors—you will need to deal with more than the matter of the theft. Flagrant cheating or theft might be a cry for help in which the teen feels she is spiraling out of control and hopes to get caught.

Whether your child has made a mistake by forgetting to take a toy out of his pocket at preschool, caused some mischief by stealing in elementary school, or has created mayhem for himself or others (stealing a car, taking it for a joy ride, and returning it seriously damaged would fit in this category), you will need to get involved to help your children develop their own sense of inner discipline.

Promoting truthfulness, integrity, and honesty is impor-tant, but we as parents must do more when our children lie, cheat, or steal. We need to step in to let them know that what they did was not right. We expect them to own what they did, fix the mess they made, and figure out how they can keep it from happening again. Holding children accountable for what they do that causes harm, what they fail to do to care, and for what they turn a blind eye to says we care deeply about them. It also says that we believe they are capable of acting with integrity, civility, and compassion. And that will require resolve on our part and discipline on theirs.

> Trust and integrity are precious resources, easily squandered, hard to regain. They can thrive only on a foundation for respect for veracity.
> —SISSELA BOK, *LYING: MORAL CHOICE IN PUBLIC AND PRIVATE LIFE*

MISTAKES, MISCHIEF, AND MAYHEM REVISITED

> One of the most enduring consequences of corporal punishments—and yet one of the least appreciated and studied—is the stifling of empathy and compassion for oneself and others. The ability to put oneself in the place of others and to understand how they feel and experience life, and the ability to grasp hurt in childhood by their parents develop immunities to empathy that often persist for a lifetime. Much pain is inflicted in the name of morality and conscience when empathy, compassion, and respect for others are absent.
> —PHILLIP GREVIN, *SPARE THE CHILD, THE RELIGIOUS ROOTS OF PUNISHMENT AND THE PSYCHOLOGICAL IMPACT OF PHYSICAL ABUSE*

Discipline, as opposed to punishment and rescuing, is one of the central themes in all of my work. A big part of raising children who can think and act ethically is our stepping in when our children have messed up so that we can help them take full ownership for what they did wrong; figure out how to keep it from happening again; and, if necessary, heal with the person they may have harmed.

The tools below will be familiar to those who know my previous writings. The mistakes, mischief, and mayhem in my first two books, *kids are worth it! Giving Your Child the Gift of Inner Discipline* and *Parenting through Crisis*, dealt with conflicts between siblings and peers, damaging property, and hurting oneself and others in anger and frustration—but not with malice or hate. What is new here is the application of these tools to ethical issues related to hoarding, harming, and hating, and how they, too, can be effectively addressed with discipline.

You are checking your four-year-old's jacket pockets before throwing it in the laundry and you find a toy dinosaur that you know is not in your child's collection. Your twelve-year-old daughter comes home with a pair of jeans you know she can't afford. Your teenage son's friend hacked into your computer and racked up a bill of $2,000 on your credit card to pay for virtual sex at a porn site.

What's a parent to do? We might be inclined to let the mistake slide—after all, the other boy has plenty of toys and won't miss this one; to punish the twelve-year-old by taking all of her jeans away and not letting her go to the mall; to ground your teenager for six months, take his computer privileges away, and ban his friend from your home forever.

These "solutions" are a variation of punishment or its alter ego, rescuing. None disciplines the kids or helps them to develop their own sense of inner discipline. And for the teenager, there is no opportunity to fix what he did, figure out how he can keep it from happening again, or heal with the people he has harmed.

How we respond to their many mistakes, occasional mischief, and rare mayhem can help provide the where-withal for our children to become responsible, resourceful, resilient, compassionate humans who feel empowered to act with integrity and a strong sense of self, or to become masters of excuses, blaming, and denial who feel powerless, manipulated, and out of control.

> Moral autonomy appears when the mind regards as necessary an ideal that is independent of all external pressure.
> —JEAN PIAGET, *THE MORAL JUDGMENT OF THE CHILD*

DISCIPLINE AND PUNISHMENT: WHY ONE WORKS AND THE OTHER ONLY APPEARS TO

> Do Justice ... love mercy ... walk humbly ...
> —MICAH, 6:8

Although the words are often used interchangeably, discipline is not synonymous with punishment. Punishment is adult-oriented, imposes power from without, arouses anger and resentment, and invites more conflict. It exacerbates wounds rather than heals them. It is preoccupied with blame and pain. It does not consider reasons or look for solutions. It is doing something *to* a child when a child behaves in a way that the parent judges to be inappropriate or irresponsible. It involves a strong element of judgment and demonstrates the parent's ability to control a child.

Punishment preempts more constructive ways of relating to a child. It drives people further apart, and it enables the parent and child to avoid dealing with the underlying causes of the problem or crisis. The overriding concerns of punishment are: What rule was broken? Who did it? And what kind of punishment does the child deserve? Punishment discourages the child from acknowledging her actions ("Wasn't me, didn't do it"). It deprives the child of the opportunity to understand the consequences of her actions, to fix what she has done, or to sympathize with the people she might have harmed. It increases tension in the home, and it helps children develop a right/wrong, good/bad distorted view of reality. "Good behavior" is bought at a terrible cost.

Punishment leaves control in the hands of the parents (sometimes literally) and gives children the message "I, as an adult, can and will make you mind," often with the rationale "for your own good." Its goal is instant obedience. Hitting a child for every item he brings home that doesn't belong to him doesn't teach him not to take property from others; it can teach him to avoid getting caught, and it can teach him that "might makes right." It becomes a tool he himself can use when his brother won't give him back his toy. Aggression begets more aggression.

More often than not, the tools used to attempt to control a child and make him "feel the pain" for what he has done are subtler than physical force. They can take the form of:

Isolation: "Bill, you are never going to set foot in this house again."

Embarrassment and humiliation: "You are not wearing jeans for the rest of the year. You will wear these worn-out pants to school."

Shaming: "If you are going to act like a three-year-old who can't be trusted with a computer, I am going to treat you like a three-year-old."

Emotional isolation: "Stay out of my sight."

Grounding: "You are grounded for six months."

Brute force: "You get one hit for every toy you took."

Illogical consequences: "I'm taking your iPod away for a month. Maybe then you will show some respect for my computer."

With these forms of punishment there is only an arbitrary connection between what the child has done and the resultant punishment. It can be a stretch for the child to try to figure out how the deed and the punishment go together. Reason suffers. As well, all of these tools can degrade, humiliate, and dehumanize children. Embarrassment, humiliation, and shaming might make a parent feel good but they are unlikely to change the behavior of the targeted child. He will probably want to hide and likely avoid taking responsibility for wrongdoing, concentrating more on how badly he is being treated than on what he did that initiated the punishment.

The mind-set of the parent is that a rule has been broken and punishment must be imposed. Under the guise of discipline, physical and emotional violence are legitimized and sanctioned. Children might behave so as not to get caught, but their sense of self-worth, their sense of responsibility, and their sense of appropriate, responsible, caring actions are seriously compromised. They often respond to punishment with the Three Fs: fright (doing as told out of dependency and fright); fight (attacking the adult or taking the anger out on others); flight (running away mentally, afraid to make a mistake or take a risk, or running away physically).

In *Living Faith*, former U.S. president Jimmy Carter speaks to the problem of relying on punishment and the resultant fear of retribution to teach children to do good. Pointing out that there are many "unenforceable standards" in our lives, he says:

> If we are interested in lives that excel, we will wish to do more than just obey the law. How do we act when there is no accountability for what we do? What restrains us from being rude to others, ignoring the plight of the needy people, giving false information when it is to our advantage, abusing a defenseless person, promulgating damaging gossip, holding a grudge, or failing to be reconciled after an argument? These are the things for which we will not be punished, and therefore the retribution is missing as a motivation.

With punishment, children are robbed of the opportunity to develop their own inner discipline and to solve their own dilemmas, the ability to act with integrity, wisdom, compassion, and mercy when there is no external accountability for what they do.

Discipline, on the other hand, is not judgmental, arbitrary, confusing, or coercive. It is not something we *do to* our children. It is working *with* our children. It is a process that gives life to their learning; it is restorative and invites reconciliation. Its goal is to instruct, teach, guide, and help children develop self-discipline—an ordering of the self from inside, not imposition from the outside. In disciplining our children, we are concerned not with mere compliance, but with inviting our children to delve deeply into themselves and reach beyond what is required or expected.

The *process* of discipline does four things the *act* of punishment cannot do:

1. It shows kids what they have done.
2. It gives them as much ownership of the problem as they are able to handle.
3. It gives them options for solving the problem.
4. It leaves their dignity intact.

For mistakes, mischief, or mayhem that intentionally or unintentionally create serious problems of great consequence, the Three Rs of reconciliation are incorporated into the four steps of discipline. These Three Rs—**restitution, resolution,** and **reconciliation**—provide the tools that are necessary to begin the healing process when serious material or personal harm has occurred. Whether it is only the four steps or the four steps and the Three Rs, discipline deals with the reality of the situation, not with the power and control of the adult. It helps change attitudes and habits that might have led to the conflict, and it promotes genuine peace in the home.

Discipline involves intervention to keep a child from further harming himself or others, or real-world consequences, or a combination of the two. Real-world consequences either happen naturally or are reasonable consequences that are intrinsically related to the child's actions. (To begin paying back the money used on the credit card would be a start in the reconciliation process.) Real-world consequences take a bit of reasoning but not a lot of energy on the parent's part, and certainly shouldn't be a struggle. Discipline by its nature requires more energy on the part of the child than on the part of the adult. If a consequence is RSVP—Reasonable, Simple, Valuable, and Practical—it will invite responsible actions from the child. If it isn't all four of these, it probably won't be effective, and it could be punishment disguised as a reasonable consequence.

Often such disguised punishment is predetermined and is based on the assumption that all violations are clear-cut. Taking anything that didn't belong to you deserves a one-size-fits-all punishment, regardless of the intent of the violator. In our rush to swift and certain judgment, there is no place for discernment of intent; the deed is seen only as a violation of a rule: children do not take what is not theirs. Even a mistake unpunished is looked upon as a possible misstep down the slippery slope to more violent deeds: "If he gets away with taking a dinosaur this time, he will probably think he can get away with stealing stuff from a store. I have to do something to him or he will think he has done nothing wrong." Such a mentality of zero-tolerance creates an environment of zero-options for parents. It is a simplistic response to complicated actions. It wrongly presumes that a young offender made the mistake, created the mischief, or caused the mayhem with the foresight, judgment, and maturity of an adult.

The opposite extreme (punishment's alter ego) is rescuing a child because we believe that children are incapable of wrongdoing with malevolent intent. We make light of the incident, ignore it entirely, or make excuses for the behavior. If we don't draw attention to it, maybe it will just go away. This is just as wrongheaded as the punitive approach. Overcome by the empathy we feel for the perpetrator, we try to convince ourselves that if we only knew the *why* of the child's misdeeds and the history that preceded the mischief or mayhem, we would be compelled to forgive and forget. Punishment ignores intent; rescuing ignores the severity of the deed.

Discipline is a more constructive and compassionate response that takes into consideration the intent, content of the deed—including its severity—circumstance, potential or actual consequences (intended and unintended), and the restorative steps needed to give life to the child's learning and to heal relationships that might have been harmed. It invites us to respond to our children with mindfulness, reason, a wise heart, compassion, and mercy, instead of just reacting with logic or emotion. It enables all of us to go beyond mere repair to restitution, resolution, and reconciliation.

Building a conscience is what discipline is all about. The goal is for a youngster to end up believing in

decency, and acting—whether anyone is watching or
not—in helpful and kind ways.
—JAMES L. HYMES, JR., "A SENSIBLE
APPROACH TO DISCIPLINE"

MISTAKES

Learn from your mistakes is an old rule, but it is
surprising how many people fail to heed it…. [I]f you
can't see the lesson in what went wrong, you're just
condemning yourself to make the same mistake again.
—CHUCK NORRIS, *THE SECRET POWER FROM
WITHIN: ZEN SOLUTIONS TO REAL PROBLEMS*

The four-year-old who took the dinosaur can return it.
The reality is that his friend has already missed it and
thinks your son took it on purpose. The problems to be
solved are (1) how to return the toy and (2) how to
demonstrate to his peer that taking it was accidental and
won't happen again. (They both stuffed all the dinosaurs
in their jacket pockets as they ran in from the rain and
dumped them into the toy bin. One was accidentally left
in your son's jacket pocket.) The preschooler can bring
the toy back to play group tomorrow and tell his friend
that he will check his pockets more carefully before he
goes home from now on. As a parent, you are there to give
your child as much ownership as he is capable of assuming
for the problem he created, offer guidelines for fixing the
mistake, and assure him that he can handle it.

For you to check your son's jacket pockets every day
before he leaves play group, or to sew up his jacket pockets
so he can't put anything in them, is to tell him nothing

about learning from his mistakes. He also learns nothing about being capable of fixing mistakes he has made or about how he can keep from making the same mistake in the future. To spank him for being careless is to invite him to become fearful of ever making another mistake, to hide his mistakes, to strike back at you if he dares, or in anger and hurt go hit his younger brother or the cat. To let him continue to take toys from play group without asking, even accidentally, is to say that he need not be concerned about any limits and boundaries. To offer excuses—"He's too young to know any better," "He didn't mean to do it," "All kids take things sometimes"—is to teach him to make excuses for his future mistakes: "It wasn't my fault." "She made me do it." "I couldn't help it."

Everyday incidents and mistakes can be opportunities for children to take ownership of problems they have created, figure out how to fix the problems, and learn how to keep the same mistake from happening again. Kids, even at age four, begin to see that when they have a problem, what they need is a good plan, not a good cover-up and not a good excuse. As they grow older, they will be less likely to dread taking risks that might result in great failure (or great success). Rather than giving up when they experience setbacks and defeats, they can be open to learning from adversity and using that knowledge to create new opportunities.

MISCHIEF

Do not find fault, find a remedy.

—HENRY FORD

The four-year-old did not intend to take the toy; the twelve-year-old intended to steal the jeans. She needs to go through all four steps of discipline with special attention to knowing how she is going to keep such theft from happening again. Taking ownership of the problem she created, she will need to return to the store and own up to what she has done. She can't return the jeans because she damaged them when she was cutting the theft tag off. She will repair the jeans herself and give them to a charity. She will need to work out a plan with the store owner to pay for the jeans, and come up with a plan that demonstrates how she can earn your trust and the store owner's trust back. The last step is making a commitment that she will not steal again. A step beyond discipline would be to discuss with her why it was so necessary to have those jeans that she would violate her own integrity; what she can do the next time she really wants something that badly; and how she can get into the practice of giving some of her clothes to those who have far less than she has.

This will involve your time as well as your child's time. Punishment is so much swifter; doing it yourself, so much smoother. However, the time you take is well worth it as your child begins to realize that all of her actions have consequences. She also learns that she is quite capable of taking full ownership of what she does, and just as capable of taking full responsibility for the problems she's created, not because she fears reprisal, but because it is the healthy thing to do.

MAYHEM

Though we want to believe that violence is a matter of
cause and effect, it is actually a process, a chain in
which the violent outcome is only one link.
—GAVIN DE BECKER, *THE GIFT OF FEAR*

Standing in your home office feeling betrayed, wronged,
hurt, disappointed, and angry, you know that discipline is
only the first step in restoring both your good credit and
the relationship you had with Bill, your son's friend who
hacked into your computer and racked up a huge credit
card debt. How easy it would be to display righteous
indignation, continue to be angry and feel victimized, to
push for punishment, seek revenge, and hold a grudge.
Just as easy and as unproductive would be to excuse the
teen or shrug your shoulders and chalk the experience up
to a once-in-a-lifetime folly that need not be addressed
further.

There is a real need for the teen to take ownership of the
mayhem he created, fix what he did, figure out how he can
keep it from happening again, and heal with the people he
has harmed. This cannot happen in an atmosphere of
punishment, vindication, or vengeance; nor will it happen in
an atmosphere of indifference. It can only happen if we are
willing to create an atmosphere of compassion, kindness,
gentleness, and patience in which we can help him work
through the four steps of discipline and the Three Rs:
restitution, resolution, and reconciliation.

RESTITUTION

Wise people seek solutions; the ignorant only cast
blame.

—TAO 79

The first R, restitution, means fixing what he did. It
involves fixing both the monetary damage and the personal
damage. The credit card debt might be easier to repair
than the personal rift created by his theft. Monetary repair
is usually less painful than the act of true repentance. And
it is only such repentance that can move him toward
reconciliation with those he has harmed by his deed. True
repentance makes no room for excuses ("I was just fooling
around"), blame-shifting ("They dared me to do it"), buts
("But you shouldn't have left your computer on"), and if
onlys ("If only my girlfriend hadn't broken up with me, I
wouldn't have needed to go to those sites"). Repentance is
not the obligatory "I'm sorry" that is used to express regret
or remorse when caught doing something wrong. To
repent honestly and unconditionally means to lament the
damage caused, not out of a sense of duty or of obligation,
but out of a *heartfelt* need to admit the wrongness of what's
been done, to express a strong sense of desire not to do it
again, to assume responsibility for the damage and begin
to mend the torn relationship.

You cannot force repentance on someone else. You can
help Bill arrive at repentance by helping him work his own
way through the Three Rs. Repentance is not a goal in itself.
Rather it is a byproduct. It comes about only as Bill works
through the whole process of reconciliation. As a wise and
caring adult who is not out to rescue or punish Bill, you can

provide the structure, the support, and the permission he needs to begin the process.

RESOLUTION

> ... there is no mystery of human behavior that cannot
> be solved inside your head or your heart.
> —GAVIN DE BECKER, *THE GIFT OF FEAR*

The second R, resolution, means figuring out a way to keep it from happening again. In other words, how can Bill create himself anew—not apart from what he has done, or in spite of what he has done, or because of what he has done? Creating anew involves integrating the past destructive act and all its results and implications into a new beginning. It happened. He can't go back and wish it not so. He needs to be able to figure out what he actually did, what he did to bring it about, what he can learn from it, what he can take from the experience to, as Ernest Hemingway described it, "become stronger in the broken places." Without such resolution, the repentance becomes a hollow regret, a mere apology to be repeated when he is caught destroying property in his next drunken rage. True repentance requires that he redirect his destructive energies in more constructive ways. It is not enough to simply say it won't happen again. Bill needs a plan and a commitment to make the plan happen.

For his plan to be effective, it must be much bigger than figuring out a way to pay back the credit card debt. His plan might need to include getting help for his sexual issues and developing a positive game plan in advance of coming to your home again. By showing your support for

Bill and his plan, you can also open the door to a frank discussion with his parents about some concerns you have about other websites he visited at your home that didn't cost a dime but could cost Bill a lot in the future.

RECONCILIATION

We have been called to heal wounds, to unite what has fallen apart, and to bring home those who have lost their way.

—ST. FRANCIS OF ASSISI

The third R, reconciliation, is a process of healing with the people you have harmed. It involves a commitment by the offender to honor his plan to make restitution and live up to his resolutions. It also involves willingness on the part of the person offended to trust, to risk, and to rebuild a relationship with the offender.

It is helpful if the offender, after making restitution, offers his time and talents to those he has harmed. This serves two purposes: one, the person harmed can experience the inherent goodness of the offender; and two, the offender can experience his own inherent goodness.

Most young offenders would not come up with this step on their own. They would like to just stop at step two and be done with the whole ordeal. It is you, the adult, who needs to push for this step, as much for yourself as for the young offender.

It will take time for you to be open to reconciling with Bill. The first night you might be in shock, hoping to wake up in the morning to find that the call from the credit card company was just a bad dream. But in the morning, you realize it is not. Your thoughts turn to revenge and your feelings to anger, or to loss and sadness, or a combination of all four. If you are honest and forthright with your thoughts and feelings, you will begin to see clearly what you are angry or sad about and what you need from Bill. Is it the wanton theft, or the fact that your privacy was violated, or the sites that were visited under your name, or a combination of all three that upsets you?

Even as you go through the motions of hearing him out with his plan to fix what he did and his resolutions, you might find yourself grieving over the loss of your privacy, the loss of trust, and the rift created by the losses. You can't just forget the incident and get on with your life as if it never happened.

To try to cover up your grief will serve neither of you well. To make light of the loss ("It was only money, that can be replaced; boys will be boys") will help you absorb the loss into yourself—and it will stay there to fester. To shrug off your own feelings ("I'm not as angry about the money and computer as I am concerned about how you are doing, Bill") is caring, but only for one party in the reconciliation. When your caring is unidirectional it says your feelings don't count, and uncounted feelings can turn into depression. An eighteenth-century monk spoke of such unbalanced caring: "Living the truth in your heart without compromise brings kindness into the world. Attempts at kindness that compromise your heart cause only sadness." Reconciliation is a two-person act.

If you will give yourself time to move through the anger and honor your sadness, you will find yourself ready to look for creative solutions to solving the problems that both you and Bill face in order to be reconciled.

Time in and of itself does not heal relationships, but it does take time to heal. Even if Bill comes to you the next day with a heartfelt apology and offer of restitution, you might need to ask for a bit more time before the two of you can truly reconcile. The *intention* behind asking for time is not to hurt him or make him suffer longer for what he did. It is time to face hurts, vent your emotions, and begin to release any grudges and destructive feelings, so that you not only reclaim your own piece of mind, you open your heart and your hands to reconciliation with Bill.

To wallow in your feelings, be they anger or sadness, is to deny yourself the opportunity of reconciling with Bill. It also locks you into viewing yourself as a helpless victim and Bill as an oppressor. You could find yourself beginning to divide your world into victims and oppressors, us and them, separate from one another and unequal. You could spend your days vengefully scheming ways to punish Bill, or spend those same days weaving your garb of victim-hood, declaring that your trust has been irrevocably broken, that anything Bill does will be too little too late. Your demands for restitution and resolution become vengeful and next to impossible. Either way, you end up stressed out, isolated, and possibly in conflict with every-one around you. The credit card debt and the hacked computer become larger than life. And your life becomes miserable. Far better to acknowledge your thoughts and your feelings, and begin to work through them to arrive at a place where you are truly ready to commit to the recon-ciliation process. Along the way, you will become freer, not unmindful of what has happened but unchained to the event.

If self-discipline and the Three Rs can become a part of your children's everyday encounters with their siblings, their peers, and the adults in their lives. They are more likely to learn from their mistakes, mischief, and mayhem and less likely to repeat them.

> History, despite its wrenching pain, cannot be unlived,
> and if faced with courage, need not be lived again.
> —MAYA ANGELOU, *ON THE PULSE OF MORNING*

REACHING OUT WITH COMPASSION AND RESTRAINT

> Nonviolence can never be equated with passivity;
> it is the essence of courage, creativity, and action.
> Nonviolence does, however, require patience: a
> passionate endurance and commitment to seek
> justice and truth no matter the cost.
> —MARY LOU KOWNACKI, *LOVE BEYOND
> MEASURE: A SPIRITUALITY OF NONVIOLENCE*

The example of the three children taking something that was not theirs went from a mistake to mischief to mayhem with increasing intent to cause harm that corresponded to increasing damage. In the real world, intent and damage don't always correspond so neatly. A simple mistake can result in serious damage, injury, or death, and an attempt to create mayhem can result in a botched armed robbery with no physical damage and no people hurt. What appears to be an accident might be well-crafted mayhem.

The mistake of not replacing a badly worn tire resulted in a brief scare on the highway and a long walk home for one teenager; for another teenager, a worn tire was the cause of a crash that killed her.

Mischief can leave a little damage and out of it can come good. The jeans were repaired and given to someone who never owed a nice pair of jeans. Mischief can also leave inconsolable grief. Leaving a school dance with a car full of friends, a seventeen-year-old driver jerked the wheel in an attempt to separate a couple who were necking in the back seat. The vehicle crossed the median and hit a van head-on. The van driver was killed and his wife and five-year-old child were seriously injured. One teen in the car was killed and one is paralyzed from the waist down. The driver is overwhelmed by the magnitude of the loss.

Planned mayhem is probably the most difficult to comprehend, to confront, and to heal from since it leaves in its wake such meaningless, preventable destruction. There was no *reason* for it to happen, only lots of empty excuses ("He made me angry," "She broke up with me so I had to take it out on someone," "She wasn't our kind"). The excuse given by one of the young men who savagely beat and tied twenty-one-year-old Matthew Shepard to a fence, leaving him to die, was that Matthew had made a pass at him. An eleven-year-old and a thirteen-year-old gun down four classmates and a teacher. A day after the killings, one boy cannot remember what happened; the other crawls into his grandmother's lap and sobs. A group of teens beat a young girl and leave her to drown in a stream. They show no remorse and blame one another for the killing.

When youngsters create mayhem intentionally, or through their mistakes and mischief at home or in the community, neither harsh punishments nor full pardon will heal the victims or the perpetrators of the mayhem. It is nonviolent engagement that is at the heart of true reconciliatory justice: the willingness to confront wrongdoing and reach out to the wrongdoer. It refuses to allow us to divide our world and our relationships into "us" and "them." It denies us the myopic vision that limits our insight. It reminds us of our connectedness with one another and can point the way out of an impasse that bitterness and hatred create.

In *Prisons that Could Not Hold: Prison Notes 1964–Seneca 1984*, Barbara Deming, a civil rights activist, speaks about how "nonviolence gives us two hands upon the oppressor— one hand taking from him what is not his due, the other slowly calming him as we do this." The one hand keeps the offender from causing more harm to self or others; the other calms the offender, allows time for reflection, and invites reconciliation. As our two hands reach out, there is at once an attempt to bring about a balance and create a tension that keeps both parties actively engaged in the reconciliatory process, as we strive to heal the rift. We are attempting to restore community.

When serious harm results from a mistake, our arm of compassion reaches the farthest, while the arm of restraint helps children acknowledge what they did to the other person, take full responsibility for these actions, confront all of their own feelings, and be open and ready to accept the feelings, the hurt, the distress, the sadness, and the anger of those who were harmed by their actions. The final two steps are to repair, as best as humanly possible, the damage that they caused and to take actions that demonstrate that they are able to rise above what they did and get on with a life that will never deny or dilute these past actions and the unintended consequences that resulted, but will not be bound and gagged by them, either.

When mischief results in mayhem, the two arms are extended equally. Compassion and restraint are both equally needed.

When a child commits intentional mayhem, the arm of restraint is the longest at the beginning of the reconciliation process, while the arm of compassion is still there.

The end goal in all three instances is an embrace in which the kids take responsibility as is warranted, are willing to make restitution, resolve to keep the mischief and mayhem from happening again, and commit to once again becoming active participants in the community. However, becoming active participants in the community may not necessarily involve having a relationship with the person who was harmed. Obviously when the person who was harmed was actually killed, there can be no relationship, as you will see with the cases of murder and genocide in the next chapter. That does not mean, however, that the perpetrator cannot go on to become a decent member of the community. Indeed, that would be one of the requirements of restorative justice.

For the youngster whose mistake or mischief has resulted in serious damage or harm, we might be inclined to offer only the arm of compassion. This will deprive the child of any opportunity to heal from within. She is likely to beat herself up emotionally, psychologically, and perhaps physically for the harm she has caused and can't fix. The driver responsible for the death of a young father and a classmate, as well as the paralysis of another classmate, needed compassion and an opportunity to make both symbolic restitution (financial) and personal restitution (service at a rehab center). The compassion extended to her by her family and other members of the community helped her get through the months before her trial. The judge provided the arm of mindfulness. A healing embrace came from the father of the teen killed in the accident.

For the youngster whose intentional acts of violence and mayhem have resulted in serious damage, irrevocable harm, or death, we might be inclined to offer neither the arm of restraint nor the arm of compassion, but rather the fist of vengeance and retribution. After the two boys, eleven and thirteen years old, shot their classmates and teacher, there were demands that the law be changed so that juveniles would have to spend the rest of their lives in prison. Some wanted the death penalty imposed.

When families and communities are faced with such violence there are often cries for swift revenge and retribution, stronger punishment and stiffer sentences; it is hoped that these solutions will somehow "fix" the problem. Effective solutions are not that simple. Reconciliation is not found in homes and societies that rely on threats and punishments as primary tools to deal with mischief and mayhem. When the main goal is to make children (or adults) "pay dearly" for what they have done, and to serve as "examples" for others who might think of doing the same, hate and bitterness find rich soil in which to grow.

In her book *Hard Questions, Heart Answers*, the Reverend Bernice A. King, daughter of slain civil rights activist Martin Luther King, Jr., explains the problem with such a retributive society:

> Those who thirst for revenge may experience the illusion of satisfaction, but it never lasts long in people of conscience because every act of violence leaves in its wake the seed of more violence.... Revenge and retribution can never produce genuine healing.

William Ayers, in his book *A Kind and Just Parent*, responded to the call for more severe punishment for young offenders by saying:

> They are kids, after all, and nothing can possibly change them into adults.... And I want to will the Court—and then all of us—to set the highest possible standard when determining judgments: "If this were my child ..." Nothing in that standard frees kids of consequences; nothing in it predetermines outcomes. It does, however, set a tone that is at once caring and complex.

This is justice rooted in deep caring. All that is done flows from this deep caring. How young offenders are treated will influence what kind of people they will grow up to be, and what kind of lives the rest of us will live. If we don't help them reconcile with the community, we could well condemn ourselves to a lifetime of fear, distrust, and mayhem.

When an entire community is committed to reconciliatory justice, young offenders are invited to rise above their misdeeds and violent acts. The goal is to mend and restore rather than isolate and punish. The search is not for vengeance but for ways to heal people and heal communities.

There is nothing as easy as denouncing. It doesn't take much to see that something is wrong, but it takes some eyesight to see what will put it right.

—WILL ROGERS

Chapter 6

Hating: Evil in Action

Hate has a nearly limitless ability to dehumanize
its victims, shutting down the most basic human
capacities for sympathy and compassion.
—RUSH W. DOZIER, JR., *WHY WE HATE:
UNDERSTANDING, CURBING, AND ELIMINATING
HATE IN OURSELVES AND OUR WORLD*

Of the three agents—hating, hoarding, and harming—
that cause damage to our selves and to our relationships
with others, hating is by far the most powerful. Hating is
destructive of our sense of community, tearing apart the
bonds we recognize in the "I and Thou" and "We." It is
evil in action.

Deep caring is the antithesis of hate. When our intent,
the driving force of our actions, is rooted in deep caring, our
actions will tend to help, not harm. And the more this
driving force becomes our way of behaving, the less likely
we will be to act cruelly when provoked, angered, tired,
frustrated, or worn out.

When deep caring is *not* a driving force in our lives, our
messy emotions and instincts (passions) can overpower both
our heart and our head. Or our head and emotions can lock
out the heart. Or our head can conjure up an entrenched

intellectual devaluation of another human being to the point where we have a cold cognitive hatred of him—no feelings one way or the other. In his research, Robert Sternberg describes three components of hate:

1. Passion: an impulsive rage, an excitement of our fear or anger, our flight-or-fight instinct (hot hate)
2. Negation of intimacy: visceral disgust (cool hate)
3. Commitment to hatred: a cognitive stance that permanently devalues the person hated (cold hate)

These can combine to create boiling hate (passion plus disgust); seething hate (cognitive plus passion); simmering hate (negation of intimacy plus commitment to hate); and the most virulent form, burning hate (rage plus disgust, plus commitment to hatred).

Hate can appear in different forms—as contempt, bigotry, degradation, exclusion, revenge, bullying. No matter which kind of hate it is, if your child is hating anyone in any way, you have some serious parenting work to do to help him or her.

CONTEMPT

> There must have been a moment at the beginning, where we all could have said no. But somehow we missed it.
>
> —TOM STOPPARD, *ROSENCRANTZ AND GUILDENSTERN ARE DEAD*

At a lecture I was giving in Calgary, Alberta, a red-haired young woman holding a dog-eared copy of *The Bully, the*

Bullied, and the Bystander approached me and said, "It was only after reading this book that I realized it was not my fault that, in grade nine, those girls held me down and set fire to my hair." Her classmates had caught her in the hallway, held her down, doused her hair with hairspray, and lit a match. The counselor, her teacher, and her parents all asked, "What did you do to make them so mad at you?" She hadn't done anything. And the other girls weren't *mad*. They had *contempt* for her.

Contempt is an attitude of utter disgust or hatred toward someone considered worthless, inferior, or undeserving of respect. Be it hot, or cold, or any variation of the two, it is guaranteed to be void of deep caring.

When people have contempt for other human beings, they can do anything to them and not feel any guilt or compassion. They can take Matthew Shepard, beat him up, tie him to a fence post, and leave him to die, and when they get arrested, excuse their actions with, "But he was gay." They can take a black man, beat him to death, drag him for two miles behind their pickup, and when arrested, shrug their shoulders and say, "Yeah, but he was black." They can throw rocks through the picture window of a family celebrating Hanukkah and declare, "But they were Jews." They can spit on a child who has a speech defect and protest, "But he has a lisp." Trip a girl and complain, "She smells." Laugh at a classmate "because he has braces." Swirl a boy's head in a toilet "for laughs; we were just kidding."

Such contempt comes packaged with three apparent psychological advantages that allow kids to harm another human being without feeling empathy, sympathy, compassion, or guilt:

1. A sense of entitlement—the privilege and right to control, dominate, subjugate, and otherwise abuse another human being.
2. An intolerance toward differences—"different" equals "inferior" and thus not worthy of respect.
3. Liberty to exclude—to bar, isolate, and segregate a person deemed not worthy of respect or care.

The biases at the foundation of this contempt are often deeply rooted attitudes found in our homes, our schools, and our society. Any bias or prejudice related to race, gender (including sexual orientation), religion, physical attributes, or mental abilities can and will be used to validate and justify contempt for an individual child or a group of children. Where children are taught to discriminate against an individual who is "different" from them, where differences are seen as "bad," and where the common bonds of our humanity are not recognized or celebrated, hate can grow.

BIGOTRY

Although the ability to form narratives may be, at some level, biological, the contents of these stories are certainly socialized. We are not born to think of people as vermin.

—ROBERT STERNBERG

For a grade nine homework assignment, a young Native girl in British Columbia was asked to read "Ten Little Indians," a poem written in 1868 by American author Septimus Winner. She complained about the poem, which begins:

"Ten little Injuns standin' in line / One toddled home and then there were nine." It goes on, one by one, to eliminate them all: number eight goes to sleep and doesn't wake up; number seven breaks his neck; number six "kicked the bucket and then there were five." The poem ends with "One little Injun livin' all alone / He got married and then there were none."

Writing for *The Globe and Mail*, Mark Hume reported that the First Nations Summit asked the British Columbia government to stop teaching this insidious and destructive poem in which at least half of the Native children die. The poem is used in the grade nine class, and also as part of the grade five curriculum to teach counting in Japanese. In researching the Ministry of Education's website, Mr. Hume found the disclaimer: "Caution. The activity sheet that accompanies the song *Ten Little Indians* on the audio cassette, depicts a stereotypical view of First Nations people."

Not only was the ministry aware of the stereotype, someone was sufficiently conscious of it to write a warning for the worksheet. Why not eliminate it completely? And why no warning about singing the song? Learning to count in Japanese using such a racist song only helps to reinforce inaccurate and hurtful stereotypes that become etched into students' consciousness alongside the language lesson. Forget empathy or sympathy; go straight to bigotry.

Just as reading and counting are lessons that children are taught, so, too, is contempt for another human being. Someone has to teach them that another person is inferior and unworthy of their respect. Some of us remember a song from the Rodgers and Hammerstein musical *South Pacific* called "You've Got to Be Carefully Taught." The song tells us that children must be taught to hate by their relatives before they are "six, seven, or eight." Its straightforward message is that hatred is not innate, but rather learned.

More often than not, young children are not instructed explicitly to consider others "inferior" or "unworthy"; these concepts are not so much *taught* as *caught*. Children pick up on your judgments, both positive and negative, by watching you relate to the store clerk, the teacher, the police officer, the clergy; hearing you speak about the new neighbor who is different, the teenager whose right ear is graced with a row of earrings, the people who celebrate religious holidays that are different from yours, the boy who has autism, the teen mom. They pick up these judgments when they feel you pull them close as you pass a homeless person on the street corner, or listen to you tell a racist or sexist joke, or see you watching a TV show and laughing at someone else's pain.

Bigotry can be caught by hearing nursery rhymes that negatively stereotype a group of people. Intolerance can be learned along with addition and subtraction. When I was in Rwanda, a parent showed me a worksheet she had to complete when she was a child in primary school in the 1960s. One of the math problems read, "If you have ten cockroaches in your town and you kill four of them, how many more do you have left to kill?" One of the cruel euphemisms for Tutsis that all elementary school children in Rwanda knew was "cockroach."

Don't Laugh at Me is a beautiful children's book that begins with a song written by Steve Seskin and Allen Shamblin and popularized by legendary folk group Peter, Paul and Mary. Accompanied by Glin Dibley's poignant illustrations, the lyrics speak of the pain of children ostracized by their peers for being different.

> I'm a little boy with glasses, the one they call a "geek."
> A little girl who never smiles cuz I got braces on my
>   teeth
> And I know how it feels to cry myself to sleep

He goes on to sing about children who are laughed at, shunned, or denigrated because of their race, religion, gender, physical or mental ability, or economic status, and he pleads:

> You don't have to be my friend but is it too much
>   to ask
> Don't laugh at me; don't call me names
> Don't get your pleasure from my pain

Children do not have to befriend every child they encounter, but they must be taught to honor the other child's humanity and treat him with dignity and regard.

To teach our children, we have to walk our talk and talk our walk so that our children "catch" us treating everyone we meet with dignity and regard, see us welcoming all sorts of people into our homes, hear us standing up for someone being beaten down and speaking out against a racist or sexist joke.

At a young age children need to be encouraged to play with a variety of children. They need to be taught to care about others, to share, and be fair; and they need to learn that you will step in immediately when you see them treat someone with disregard or scorn, or hear them laugh at someone else's pain.

Degradation: Hazing

Hazing is based on humiliation and degradation.
—ANTHONY MASI, INTERIM PROVOST,
UNIVERSITY OF MCGILL

We have to wonder why it is considered "fun and exciting" to demean another human being. We speak out of both sides of our mouth when we tell children not to bully one another on the playground, then encourage or condone hazing, calling it "character building" and "just part of the game."

In the fall of 2005, an eighteen-year-old varsity football player at McGill University in Montreal came forward to allege that he had been sexually assaulted by a veteran player during a team initiation, while other players cheered. McGill, one of Canada's oldest and most distinguished universities, suspended several players and canceled the rest of the football season. Anthony Masi, the interim provost, announced that "there was no evidence that anyone was sodomized," but that the initiation did include "nudity, degrading positions and behaviors, gagging, touching in inappropriate manners with a broomstick, as well as verbal and physical intimidation of rookies by a large part of the team."

Although the student who came forward was applauded by the university, the team's quarterback was not so accommodating to the boy who refused to be so accommodating to the humiliation and degradation: "Obviously something went wrong with this one individual. He took something the wrong way, and to this day, we don't know why or what. Something obviously is wrong if he's the only person who's ever had a problem. I went through initiation ... it was along the same lines." Along the same lines as nudity, degrading positions and behaviors, gagging, touching in an inappropriate manner with a broomstick, as well as verbal and physical intimidation, and the quarterback thinks there is something wrong with the player who objected. He seems to believe that, as long as it is an "initiation," he can justify almost any type of behavior, no matter how abusive.

The culture of hazing actually changes the person involved in the interactions. A young girl who was seriously injured in a powderpuff football hazing incident was actually looking forward to "having a crack at the initiates next year." Her mother was stunned at the change in her daughter's attitude toward her teammates, bonding with those who harmed her, and now ready to do harm to the next group of initiates.

It is important for all of us to feel that we belong. It can be such a powerful force for young people that they will do unspeakable and cruel things to themselves and others to be accepted into a group. Rites of initiation can be powerful and meaningful. They do not have to be humiliating or demeaning.

In the August 2000 national survey on high school hazing conducted by Alfred University, principal investigator Nadine C. Hoover explained, "When initiation rites are done appropriately, they meet teenagers' needs for a sense of belonging, and the group's needs for members to understand the history and culture of the group, and build relationships with others who belong. Initiation rites are comprised of pro-social behaviors that build social relationships, understanding, empathy, civility, altruism, and moral decision making."

EXCLUSION: A CLOSED CIRCLE

> We hadn't quarreled about anything, or fallen out
> over hurtful words, but he had already expelled me
> from his circle.
> —INNOCENT, A TUTSI, SPEAKING OF HIS NEIGHBOR
> AND *GÉNOCIDAIRE*, IN *MACHETE SEASON*

In the movie *Chocolat*, a close-knit community is confronted
with newcomers who are not like them. The townspeople
are getting ready for Lent, preparing to give up certain
activities they enjoy, deny themselves foods they like, and
resist temptations to sin—all with the intention of behaving
in a more "Christ-like" fashion. They are anything but that,
however, when confronted with these people who dress
oddly, speak weirdly, and act differently.

Distressed by the church-goers' behavior toward these
newcomers, Père Henri chucks his planned Easter sermon
and preaches instead: "I think we can't go around measuring
our goodness by what we don't do, by what we deny
ourselves, what we resist, and who we exclude. I think we've
got to measure goodness by what we embrace, what we
create, and who we include."

The people in the village are not callous or uncaring
toward one another; they just don't see the outsiders as
worthy of that *same* respect, fairness, or compassion. They,
in essence, wall them off and keep them out of their circle of
caring.

The more our circle of caring shrinks, and the higher
we build the walls, the more likely it is that our indifference to those outside our circle will translate into a vicious
cycle of violence against those we have excluded, with no

fear of retaliation or rebuke from our neighbors who are walled in with us. But *Chocolat*'s priest, Père Henri, refuses to stay within those walls. So does the lawyer Atticus Finch in *To Kill a Mockingbird*. When asked why he is willing to defend a man nobody else in the community thinks he should be defending, he replies, "Because, first I must live with myself. And the one thing that does not abide by majority rule is a person's conscience."

REVENGE: RUN UPON RUIN

You cannot be fueled by bitterness. It can eat you up but it cannot drive you.

—BENAZIR BHUTTO

Some young people "run upon ruin" in an attempt to avenge themselves of some slight or insult. Their own self-regard and their regard for others are secondary to their desire to get even. An inclination to let their passions have free range can create hot hate. With this passion running the show, their disposition is more likely to be hair-triggered, brought on by the slightest provocation. When situations interact with such a disposition to produce an action, that action is more likely to be destructive than helpful.

Questioned about some missing shot glasses, Lucky Iromuanya stormed out of an end-of-the year party at the home of two University of Nebraska soccer players. The twenty-three-year-old returned a short time later with a gun. Aiming at a man trying to calm him down, Lucky shot once. The single bullet passed through Nolan Jenkins's scalp before exiting and striking Nebraska soccer standout Jenna

Cooper in the throat. Jenna died the next day. In one instant many lives were radically altered, and one was senselessly lost. Had Lucky even acted more out of self-interest, anticipating his own personal ruin (a life sentence) and the death of a peer (a death he would have to live with the rest of his life), he could perhaps have checked his desire for revenge.

That same spring in Arvada, Colorado, another young man crashed a party with several carloads of fellow gang members. As eighteen-year-old Garry McLaughlin stood in the driveway of his home making sure the gang members left, twenty-year-old Patrick Suchaiya fired several shots, one hitting Garry and killing him. Garry died trying to protect his fifteen-year-old sister. Patrick, described by his family as "a sweet, caring boy who put others' needs above his own," was sentenced to seventy-three and a half years in prison. His lawyer said he was remorseful. His conscience had kicked in after the fact, and too late to be of any good to Garry or his family. Patrick did not put anyone's needs above his own, and he showed no care or concern for the teenager as he killed him.

Speaking to Sue Lindsay, a *Rocky Mountain News* reporter, Garry's stepfather, County District Judge Jack Berryhill, shared his thoughts on the impact of Garry's death on the family. "There is no such thing as closure for such a tragedy. What an odd concept really, as if we could close the door on our pain. Closure is for business deals, not for feelings for people that we love. We will never get over the loss." Normal life has forever changed for the family, he said. "Normal is having tears waiting behind every smile. Normal is every happy event always backed up with sadness lurking close behind because of the hole in our hearts. Normal is trying not to cry all day. Every family gathering will always be a reminder of the one who isn't there."

Revenge is the result of passions overcoming our head and our heart, trumping our deep caring, resulting in hot hate. For the Cooper and Berryhill families, piercing grief, intense sorrow, and sadness that will forever temper joy are the passages of grief they will circle through the rest of their lives because in one moment someone sought revenge.

> It's not so much conscious, premeditated evil as it is self-centered disregard for the rest of the human race, for the little people on whose shoulders we all stand, for the evil effects of our lives on the lives of others.
> —JOAN CHITTISTER, *IN SEARCH OF BELIEF*

BULLYING

> How fragile are the bonds of civility and decency that keep any kind of human community from utter collapse.
> —RABBI RICHARD L. RUBENSTEIN

My third book, *The Bully, The Bullied, and The Bystander*, was about three characters in the tragedy known as bullying. Bullying is about malice and hate. None of us wants to think our child is treating others with contempt, but sometimes it is necessary to accept this as the truth. The punch your son gave his classmate was not born of anger or frustration. It came from calculated aggression; he displayed an air of indifference as he calmly explained that his playmate was a wimp. The teacher called to say that your daughter led a group of girls in tormenting a new girl in the lunchroom and refused to let her sit at their table. No, it was not playful teasing, and yes, it was *your daughter* who was leading the group. You overhear your son and his friends laughing at what they did to the boy who was in a wheelchair. Your daughter calls another girl in your neighborhood a slut. She says that's the way all kids her age talk—where have you been?

Terrorizing, intimidating, shunning, tormenting, and ridiculing are not behaviors that fall within the ordinary boundaries of sibling rivalry or peer conflicts. They are acts of contempt—conscious, willful, deliberate, hostile activities intended to harm. It is important that you not make light of what happened and write it off as the "usual stuff" between siblings or playmates. Nor do you want to try to justify, rationalize, or minimize your child's behavior ("That boy is obnoxious; he asked for it," "Girls will be girls—we all did that at her age," "They didn't mean to hurt his feelings; they were just teasing"). Letting her get away with such behavior does not serve her well. You are subtly saying that you don't expect much from her, thus giving her a ready-made excuse for such cruel practices.

Can a child feel guilty about what he has done? Yes, but he can't be punished or shamed into feeling guilty or remorseful. Those feelings must come from the inside. It is important to feel guilty about something done intentionally to harm another. That's what having a conscience is all about. But the feeling of guilt won't be there unless empathy and sympathy have been nurtured.

We saw earlier that even infants experience "empathic distress" when they see another baby suffering, in grief, or in pain. This feeling is at the root of a sense of "healthy guilt." When a child has to attend to the consequences of his actions (or inactions) with the one he has harmed, he experiences healthy guilt and engages his conscience. Bigotry, prejudice, and hatred can all contribute to the extinguishing of this spark of empathy, until a child becomes capable of getting pleasure from another's pain, inflicting the pain to get that pleasure, or having an apathetic response to another's pain.

Empathy, sympathy, and guilt go hand in hand. Your son must care about the feelings of others before he can feel guilty about hurting them or treating them unfairly. Your role is not to shame him, it is to let him know that what he did was wrong and that you care enough about him to help him make it right.

If you know your child is being mean and cruel to her siblings, you will need to act immediately and decisively. Consider your own behavior. Is there anything you are doing to encourage or support such cruelty? If the answer is yes, you can change your attitudes, behaviors, and habits. In turn, you will change your relationship with your child, which in turn will affect the way she relates to her peers and siblings.

If the answer is no, there could be other socializing influences that are giving rise to your child's cruelty—peer relationships, or social and educational environments such as daycare and school. Having disregard, loathing, or hatred for someone are states of mind and heart that are learned.

Just as your child was capable of being disrespectful, malicious, and callous, so is she capable of being respectful, kind, and compassionate. She learned to be mean; she can learn more positive ways to act with her peers with civility and common decency. In *The Bully, The Bullied, and The Bystander*, I wrote at length about ways to help your child rewrite her bullying script and assume a new, more compassionate role. In summary, there are seven steps you can take:

1. Intervene immediately with discipline (including restitution, resolution, and reconciliation)—not punishment.
2. Create opportunities for your child to "do good"—to care, share, and help.
3. Nurture empathy and sympathy.
4. Teach friendship skills—assertive, respectful, and peaceful ways to relate to others.
5. Closely monitor your child's TV viewing, video game playing, computer activities, and music. (They do not cause cruelty, but they can help create a culture of "mean.")
6. Engage your child in more constructive, entertaining, and energizing activities—cruise a river instead of cruising the school hallways to find someone to harm; climb a rock wall instead of trampling over a peer.
7. Teach your child to "will good"—to speak up and do the right thing when the burden is heavy.

Caring deeply about others would prevent your son from coldly and callously harming his classmate, or prevent your daughter from maliciously twisting her brother's arm. They would both be able to see other children as worthy of the same regard as they, and be able to look ahead to see what pain their actions would cause for other children. They would also be more willing to stand up and speak out when anyone else was treating another child unfairly or unjustly.

Kids who are mean and cruel to their peers tend to be less able to see from another's perspective. They tend to see things exclusively from their own point of view and to be concerned only about their own feelings. The language is: "You will give me what I want; I don't care how you feel," or, "I do care how you feel: the worse, the better."

Your child can learn to recognize his siblings' or peers' sadness, hurt, or dejection and identify with their distress. He can also learn to imagine how it would feel if he were in their shoes and know how to extend kindness and help. You can begin to help him by sharing your own feelings, explaining why you feel the way you do, responding with loving-kindness and compassion, helping him become aware of how his hurtful behavior affects others, teaching him principled moral prohibitions against hurting others, and helping him develop his ability to adopt other perspectives.

Feelings and thoughts lead to action. By using everyday situations, you can teach your child first to recognize and label his feelings and identify his thoughts: "How did you feel when you failed the exam?" "How did you feel when you helped your teammate score the goal?" "How did you feel when you tipped that boy's wheelchair over?" "How did you feel when you helped your sister?" "How did you feel when you twisted your brother's arm?" "What were your thoughts about your teammate scoring the goal?"

Your next step is to help him take another person's perspective—to both imagine what it would be like to be in the other person's shoes, to feel what the other person felt, and to think about what the other person thought.

Following that, you can help him to recognize his own feelings and thoughts and take on the other person's perspective *before* he acts. "What did you feel before you tipped the wheelchair? The next time you have those feelings, what can you do with them that will eliminate the possibility of your classmate being hurt by your actions? What can you do with those feelings that is more constructive?" "What did you feel before you twisted your brother's arm? What can you do the next time you feel that way?" "What was it you felt you needed? How can you get what you need without hurting someone else?" "Can you imagine what the other child would think and feel if you called him such ugly names?" "Is there another way that you could tell him what is bothering you?" "Would you want that said to you if you were in his shoes?" "What else could you do with your thoughts and feelings that would acknowledge your own wishes and still respect the dignity and worth of the other child?"

ABSENCE OF CARING

The only conclusion I can reach is that we are in desperate need of a transfusion of humanity. If we believe that all humans are human, then how are we going to prove it? It can only be proven through our actions.

—LIEUTENANT-GENERAL ROMÉO DALLAIRE, *SHAKE HANDS WITH THE DEVIL: THE FAILURE OF HUMANITY IN RWANDA*

In writing of how hate promotes an emotional coldness and helps create the stark outlines of genocide, Rush W. Dozier, Jr., stated, "Hate at its most atrocious annihilates mercy and feeds on the infliction of pain and death."

In the process of putting their bigotry, intolerance, and hatred into action, children become so desensitized that they minimize or normalize their indifference, callousness, and malice. Add to this deadly mix getting pleasure from another person's pain. When we adults write off our children's behavior as "boys will be boys," "girls will be girls," we, too, contribute to this normalization and pleasure without guilt. When we fuel our children's hatred with our own intolerance, bigotry, and hatred, we set the scenes captured in two photographs that Alfie Kohn keeps on his desk and wrote about in his book *The Brighter Side of Human Nature*.

The first is a young girl wearing a T-shirt bearing the message "Thank God for AIDS." Kohn writes that he looks at the photo long and often, looking for clues to explain the girl's feelings, the parents' bigotry. He can only assume that she has never known a homosexual, or a person dying of an incurable disease: "[B]ut something other than a simple lack of experience is at work here and I am not entirely sure I know what it is."

The second photo was reproduced from a scholarly article on dehumanization. It shows a Southern lynch mob, a crowd of white men and women standing in front of the bodies of two black men hanging from a tree:

> Eight or nine of the white people are facing the
> camera, several of them smiling as if they were at
> a picnic; one man points with his index finger so

the viewer should be sure not to miss the two dead men or his own satisfaction with what had been done to them. In the lower left ... stands a young couple. They are both looking at me and grinning ... She is holding her right hand behind her back and he is grasping her thumb affectionately.

Kohn asks how this can be: "How can these people be casual, relaxed, *pleased* when two corpses ... are swinging from a linden tree not fifteen feet away?" Kohn calls this "the logical conclusion of failing to appreciate the humanity one shares with members of an out-group."

There is "something other than a simple lack of experience at work here," and the answer to how these people can be "casual, relaxed, *pleased*," is one word: hate. Failure to appreciate the humanity one shares with a member of the out-group is the foundation of that hate. It is the failure to honor our common "We," and our "I and Thou." Once the other becomes an "it," a "them against us," an "enemy," "collateral damage," a "cockroach," "vermin," there is no need to respond with loving-kindness or compassion. Lynch mobs, like those in Alfie Kohn's picture, often posed for the camera. They showed no fear of being identified, because they knew no white jury—in other words, no one in their own circle—would convict them.

Hate is not the opposite of deep caring; it is the absence of deep caring.

If you have an attitude of superiority, it is very hard to think wiser.

—ROBERT STERNBERG

NONVIOLENCE AS A WAY OF LIFE

I must stand and speak for those who have no voice
and those who are most vulnerable. It is never the
right time, it is never convenient, but if not now,
when?

—DR. BYRON PLUMLEY, JUSTICE EDUCATION
COORDINATOR, REGIS UNIVERSITY

Willingness to take a stand, and perhaps stand alone, is
sometimes what it takes to begin to enlarge our circle of
caring, to break down the walls that keep some people
outside the perimeter. Rosa Parks, a civil rights hero and
catalyst for the Montgomery Bus Boycott, sat down and
refused to get up when told to relinquish her seat to a white
man. It was her stand against intolerance, bigotry, and
hatred. "The time had just come when I had been pushed as
far as I could stand to be pushed, I suppose. They placed me
under arrest. And I wasn't afraid. I don't know why I wasn't,
but I didn't feel afraid. I had decided that I would have to
know once and for all what rights I had as a human being
and a citizen, even in Montgomery, Alabama."

Our children must see us as more than non-bigoted, non-
racist, or non-sexist. We must show them that we are *anti*-
bigoted, *anti*-racist, *anti*-sexist, actively involved in our
community working against such intolerance and hatred and
standing up for social justice.

A classmate and friend of mine, Dr. Byron Plumley,
was arrested on Sunday, November 17, 2002, at Georgia's
Fort Benning army base with four of his students from
Regis University in Denver, Colorado. Participating in a
nonviolent demonstration to close the Western Hemisphere

Institute for Security Cooperation (formerly the School of the Americas—SOA), he, along with eighty-nine other people, was arrested that day for walking onto the army base. Plumley's students received fines, but he was fined and sentenced to jail. In preparation for trial he wrote to his friends a statement called "Silence is Complicity." In it he spoke of using civil disobedience as a vehicle for participation in democracy. Both a burden and an opportunity, he saw that at the risk of his liberty, he had greater possibilities for voicing critical issues:

> Over the past thirty years my teaching has been an integration of faith and justice. My classes have focused on the lives and teachings of Jesus, Gandhi, Day, King and Chavez among many other spiritually rooted nonviolent social activists. My teaching is not only historical and theoretical. Personal integrity demands that I give witness to the life and action of those who have called us to live with compassion and justice. Nonviolence is a way of life demonstrated in action and I must walk my talk.

The silence he spoke of was to him, and to all of us who oppose the human rights violations of the SOA, simply a luxury that allows the suffering in so many South American countries to continue. As he mentioned in his letter, so many human rights workers, health care workers, teachers, and religious personnel in these countries were not afforded the luxury of a six-month jail term. They were tortured and murdered, including Archbishop Oscar Romero, American church women, and six Jesuit priests, along with their house-keeper and her daughter, by people trained at the SOA.

NOT IN OUR TOWN

We can all do something.
—ARCHBISHOP OSCAR ROMERO

In December 1993, Billings, Montana, entered a "white supremacist hell." Jewish graves were vandalized. Native American homes were sprayed with epithets like "Die Indian." When skinheads lobbed a chunk of cinderblock through a window that displayed a menorah, the police suggested to Tammie Schnitzer that she remove all Jewish symbols from the outside of her home. Her refusal to be bowed by the hate-filled actions of a few was reported in *Ten Ways to Stop Hate:*

> As if suddenly aware of hate in its midst, Billings responded. Vigils were held. Petitions were signed. A painter's union led 100 people in repainting houses. Within days, the town erupted in meno-rahs—purchased at K-Mart, Xeroxed in church offices, and printed in the *Billings Gazette*—displayed in thousands of windows…. Mrs. Schnitzer took her son for a ride through town to look at all the menorahs.
>
> "Are they Jewish, too?" a wide-eyed Isaac asked.
>
> "No," she said, "they're friends."
>
> The manager of a local sporting goods store, Rick Smith, was so moved by events that he

changed the sales pitch on his street marquee....
[H]e mounted, in foot-high letters: "Not in Our
Town. No Hate. No Violence. Peace on Earth."

These words on the marquee provided the slogan for a
movement orchestrated by The Working Group, a non-
profit production company that produced the video "Not in
Our Town."

The answers, I now believe, are as complex as the
human soul ... one reason why there is no one
explanation for evil and no one form of justice to
combat it."
                —ELIZABETH NEUFFER, *THE KEY TO MY NEIGHBOUR'S*
                      HOUSE: SEEKING JUSTICE IN BOSNIA AND RWANDA

THE GOOD SAMARITAN—A LESSON ON COMPASSION

Five ways of moving toward unswerving attitude of
service: be authentic, be vulnerable, be accepting, be
present, be useful.
                —JAMES A. AUTRY, *THE SERVANT LEADER*

A man was set upon by robbers, beaten, and left in a ditch to
die. A priest and a Levite, both respected religious leaders,
saw the man and passed by him. For them, the ritual prohi-
bition against touching a dead body trumped compassion. It
was an outsider, the Samaritan, who stopped, poured oil and
salve into the man's wounds, lifted him up onto his own
donkey, took him to an inn, and paid the innkeeper to care
for him.

In August 2005, Hurricane Katrina devastated the city of New Orleans, killing over a thousand people and dislocating hundreds of thousands more. At a prayer service for the victims of the hurricane, Bishop T. J. Jakes spoke about the five truths found in *The Parable of the Good Samaritan:*

1. *Restoration is more than observation.* To care is to *do* something.
2. *We must move beyond our neighborhoods.* Our neighbors are more than those who look like us.
3. *We cannot help people if we exalt ourselves.* The Samaritan found the victim on the ground. We have to care enough to be willing to come down to where the pain and poverty is; and love enough to trade places with them, to walk in their shoes.
4. *We need resources not rhetoric.* It is not so important what we say as what we do; what we are willing to *share* and how we are willing to *help*.
5. *Relationships are productive.* The Samaritan knew the innkeeper and called upon him to help the man who was robbed. "We must be able to communicate beyond our divides; to build bridges between perspectives and ideas. You can't multiply by dividing, you can't add by subtracting. We must build a bridge between black and white and brown, between left and right."

These five points make up a hand that must reach out and help those in need. Bishop Jakes called upon those listening to "stretch forth that helping hand."

In a true Samaritan story during that hurricane, Steve Miller, imprisoned on forgery charges in the Hancock

County jail in Bay St. Louis, Missouri, rescued several people from the floodwaters. When the hurricane hit, prisoners were able to flee the jail. As he was leaving, he heard the cries of two elderly women trapped in their home. He pulled both to safety and took off his shirt to make a sling for one of them who had a broken arm. He went on to dig out an elderly man from the debris. Steve rode to the hospital in the back of the pickup using his hand to keep the rain off the face of the seriously injured man.

When interviewed after the storm, Steve said, "I'm glad I did something good like this. I've never done anything like this before." When asked how he would feel if he didn't get a pardon from the governor for his forgery, he answered, "If I don't get it I won't be mad. I already feel better about myself."

It is in us to care, and when we do, we are changed.

We see things not as they are but as we are.

—ANAIS NIN

GRIEVING DAD SPURNS HATRED

But the words of my Seneca mother to me when I was badly wronged and wanted revenge and retaliation stay with me: "Do not be so ignorant and stupid and inhuman as they are. Go to the elder and ask for the medicine that will turn your heart from bitterness to sweetness. You must learn the wisdom of how to let go of poison."

—SISTER JOSÉ HOBDAY

After his daughter, Julie Marie, was killed in the Oklahoma City bombing, Bud Welch just wanted to see the killer or killers "fry." However, almost two years later, Stephanie Salter from the *San Francisco Examiner* reported that the same Bud Welch who had wanted the convicted bomber, Timothy McVeigh, to pay with his own life had traveled over two thousand miles to spend time with Timothy McVeigh's father, Bill, and sister, Jennifer. In a phone interview with Ms. Salter, Bud Welch spoke of his journey toward reconciliation. "When I got ready to leave, Jennifer hugged me and then she just took to sobbing. I put my hands on her cheeks, and held her face and said, 'Honey, the three of us are in this together for the rest of our lives. We can make the most of it if we choose. I don't want your brother to die, and I will do what I can to help.'"

Those two thousand miles were a short jaunt compared to the long road his heart had traveled from April 19, 1995, the day his daughter and the 167 other people were killed in the bomb blast of the Alfred P. Murrah Federal Building. For several months he was filled with rage, revenge, and hate, wanting those responsible to pay with their own lives. Then one cold January day he started to think about how miserable he was. "I was smoking three packs of cigarettes a day and drinking too much, and I didn't like myself. I wanted to know: After they were tried and executed, how was that going to help me?… I finally realized, it ain't going to help me at all. It sure won't bring Julie Marie back. Revenge, hatred, and rage—that's why Julie Marie is dead today."

Seeing the pain on the face of Bill McVeigh at the trial, Bud Welch wanted to tell him face to face that he cared about what this father of the man who killed his daughter was going through.

There are many who don't agree with him and have actually distanced themselves from him: some simply believe in their heart of hearts that retribution is the only way to go; others seem fearful that his presence might diminish their thirst for revenge. Perhaps they fear that losing their thirst for revenge would in some way dishonor the dead, and leave them with nothing but a pain-racked heart. For others, their hatred is now embedded in their hearts and permeates their whole lives. They are not in possession of their hatred; their hatred now possesses them.

What Bud Welch came to know on his journey is that letting go of the need for revenge does not reduce the horror of the deed, does not excuse it, tolerate it, cover it, or smother it. He looked horror in the face, called it by name, let it choke and enrage him, but his anger is now without hatred. "People still think you can get closure or healing from revenge, but you can't. I've had a really deep hole in my heart since Julie was killed. A big chunk of me is just gone forever. But killing Tim McVeigh is not going to grow the chunk back." He has taken the energy of his anger and used it to fight the death penalty; he now believes that vengeance has been tried for too long and has produced only more violence and revenge.

Timothy McVeigh declared the bombing of the federal building to be retaliation for the U.S. bombings in Iraq and the Waco, Texas, killings. He was executed on June 11, 2001. He never repented publicly for what he did. When asked about the children who died in the Murrah Building's childcare center, he said that they were "collateral damage."

This comment shocked many Americans. It was no accident that he used that term. Timothy McVeigh was a decorated war veteran from the first Persian Gulf War. Government officials used that same term, "collateral damage," when describing the death of children in a bombing raid during that war. Timothy McVeigh had told friends that he was haunted by the deaths of those children in the desert and the two men he killed in combat. What Bud Welch understood, unlike Timothy McVeigh and the politicians who try to mask reality with euphemisms, is that vengeance leads only to violence, revenge, and heartaches that don't go away—ever.

> … you wake up one day and for the first time in a long time, you are not encased in ice.
> —ISMAR SCHORSCH

A NOBEL PEACE PRIZE, A GOOD FRIDAY AGREEMENT, AND A SCHOOL

> The man who opts for revenge should dig two graves.
> —CHINESE PROVERB

On Friday, October 16, 1998, Catholic pacifist John Hume and Protestant David Trimble, onetime hardliner and unionist, were jointly awarded the Nobel peace prize for their efforts to bring about peace and reconciliation in Northern Ireland. Both men took part in the creation of the Good Friday Peace Agreement signed in April of that year and overwhelmingly approved in May by voters on both sides of the conflict. Both men acknowledged that the agreement was a small step in the reconciliation process and that much more compromise and healing would be needed before lasting peace could be achieved. Just as in other countries racked by terrorism and violent discord, there is a need for the process of reconciliatory justice if the cycle of vengeance is to be stopped.

As part of the Northern Ireland Good Friday Peace Agreement's promise to release more than four hundred convicted members of the Irish Republican Army and pro-British paramilitary, Thomas McMahon, an IRA bomb-maker sentenced to life in prison, was set free shortly after the agreement was signed. It was McMahon who had planted the bomb that destroyed a yacht in 1979, killing Lord Mountbatten, the great-uncle of England's Prince Charles, along with Mountbatten's fourteen-year-old grandson, Nicolas, eighty-three-year-old Lady Brabourne, and fifteen-year-old boatsman Paul Maxwell while they sailed near Mullaghmore, in western Ireland.

According to a news report written by Shaun Pogatchnik of the Associated Press, the release of the convicted bomber stirred outrage among many in Ireland and England. Outrage was noticeably missing, however, from the statement given by John Maxwell, father of the fifteen-year-old killed in the attack.

"Keeping him in prison will, unfortunately, not bring my son back. Peace is the imperative now and we must look forward, so that perhaps Paul's death and those of thousands of others from both sides of the political divide here will not have been entirely in vain…. McMahon should not be kept in prison for the sake of revenge."

This was not the first time that John Maxwell had looked forward since the death of his son. No matter how willing he was to let go of a need for revenge, John Maxwell daily faced the fact that the death of his son was forever a reality. Instead of letting his anger and frustration turn to hatred toward Thomas McMahon, he decided to take that energy and use it to fight the beast of terrorism. Education was his weapon of choice. He helped found an elementary school in Enniskillen, Northern Ireland, a school in which Catholics and Protestants are taught together.

Sharing the Nobel Peace Prize with David Trimble, John Hume emphasized the role both empathy and sympathy have played in bringing peace to one of the world's explosive cauldrons of hate. "We have to realize that our common humanity transcends our differences.... The real border is not between north and south, but in the minds and hearts of our people."

> To love, and bear; to hope till Hope creates
> From its own wreck the thing it contemplates;
> Neither to change, nor falter, nor repent;
> This, like the glory, Titan, is to be
> Good, great and joyous, beautiful and free.
> —PERCY BYSSHE SHELLEY, *PROMETHEUS UNBOUND*

MURDER AND TRANSFORMATION

You've done something terrible perhaps, but you're also a human being with a mind and a heart and a soul, and you've got to find a way to live beyond the worst thing you have ever done.
> —FRANK TOBIN, TEACHER IN THE JUVENILE
> JUSTICE SYSTEM IN CHICAGO

In the book *Jewish Wisdom*, Rabbi Joseph Telushkin retells a story first told by George Herald in "My Favorite Assassin," published in *Harper's*, April 1943. The story is about Ernst Werner Techow, a German right-wing terrorist, who, along with two others, assassinated Germany's Jewish foreign minister, Walter Rathenau, in 1922. The motivations for the crime included both political extremism and anti-Semitism. All three assassins were arrested. Techow's two accomplices committed suicide. Mathilde Rathenau, the mother of the murdered man, wrote to Techow's mother:

> In grief unspeakable, I give you my hand—you of all women the most pitiable. Say to your son that, in the name of the spirit of him he has murdered, I forgive, even as God may forgive, if before an earthly judge your son makes a full and frank confession of his guilt … and before a heavenly judge repents. Had he known my son, the noblest man earth bore, he would have rather turned the weapon on himself. May these words give peace to your soul. Mathilde Rathenau.

Techow was released from prison for good behavior after five years. In 1940, when France surrendered to Nazi Germany, he smuggled himself into Marseilles where he helped over seven hundred Jews escape to Spain with Moroccan permits. Techow helped the wealthy and the penniless alike.

Shortly before his activities in Marseilles, Techow met a nephew of Rathenau, and confided that his repentance and transformation had been triggered by Mathilde Rathenau's letter: "Just as Frau Rathenau conquered herself when she wrote that letter of pardon, I have tried to master myself. I only wished I would get an opportunity to right the wrong I have done."

Even after saving over seven hundred Jews, Techow knew there was nothing he could do to ever truly "right the wrong" he had done. Rabbi Walter Rathenau was dead. Nothing Techow could say would alter that, and no matter how many Jews he later saved it would not change the reality that murder "cannot be undone nor pardoned."

Just as Ernst Werner Techow realized he could not "right the wrong," others who have killed have made similar comments. Jean-Baptiste, a convicted perpetrator in the genocide in Rwanda, knew he, too, would have to live with the awful reality of what he had done to not just one person but many Tutsi: "There is now a crack in my life. I don't know about the others. I don't know if it is because of my Tutsi wife. But I do know that the clemency of justice or the compassion of the stricken families can never fix this crack. Even the resurrection of the victims might not fix it. Perhaps not even my death will fix it."

A QUESTION OF FORGIVENESS

We who suffered in those dreadful days, we who cannot obliterate the hell we endured, are forever being advised to keep silent.

—SIMON WIESENTHAL, *THE SUNFLOWER,*
ON THE POSSIBILITIES AND LIMITS OF FORGIVENESS

While imprisoned in a Nazi concentration camp, Simon Wiesenthal was taken one day from his work detail to the bedside of a young Catholic Nazi soldier. Haunted by his killing of Jews, the soldier wanted to confess to—and obtain forgiveness and absolution from—a Jew. Any Jew would do. The Nazi needed to confess "in order to save his soul."

Wiesenthal listened patiently for hours as this young man described the crimes in which he participated. He even swatted a fly from the soldier's bandaged head. When the soldier asked for his forgiveness in the name of all the Jews he had harmed or killed, Simon Wiesenthal walked out of the room.

Wiesenthal survived the war and went to work for the U.S. Army gathering evidence for the Nazi war crimes trials. He dedicated most of his life to seeking information on and tracking down fugitive Nazis, so that they could be brought to justice. In his book *The Sunflower, On the Possibilities and Limits of Forgiveness,* he describes how the accused at their trials rarely showed remorse, regretting only that witnesses had survived to tell their tales. He then asks the reader and himself, "Was my silence at the bedside of the dying Nazi wrong?" He imagines how the soldier might have behaved if he had survived to be put on trial:

> Would he have spoken in court as he did to me before he died in the Dean's room? Would he openly admit what he had confessed on his deathbed? Perhaps the picture that I formed of him in my mind was kinder than reality.... How could I have known if he would have committed further crimes had he survived?

I have a fairly detailed knowledge of the life story of many Nazi murderers. Few of them were born murderers. They had been mostly peasants, manual laborers, clerks, or officials, such as one meets in normal everyday life. In their youth they had received religious instruction; and none of them had a previous criminal record. Yet they became murderers, expert murderers by conviction. It was as if they had taken down their SS uniforms from the wardrobe and replaced them with their consciences as well as with their civilian clothes.

Wiesenthal invites those reading the book to be challenged by the question he poses "just as much as it once challenged my heart and my mind. There are those who can appreciate my dilemma, and so endorse my attitude, and there are those who will be ready to condemn me for refusing to ease the last moment of a repentant murderer."

In all of these stories, none of the perpetrators asked for forgiveness, except the young Nazi soldier, and none of those in a position to forgive, except Mathilde Rathenau (who forgave in the spirit of her son), mentioned forgiveness. Even Jean-Baptiste, a perpetrator, used the words "compassion of the stricken families."

And what about reconciliation? Mathilde Rathenau did not reconcile with her son's murderer. She offered him forgiveness in her son's name. John Maxwell did not reconcile with his son's murderer. He built a school. Bud Welch did not reconcile with his daughter's murderer. He spurned hatred and revenge and worked against the death penalty. Simon Wiesenthal remained silent and walked away. He spent the rest of his life hunting down Nazi war criminals. None of these people sought reconciliation with the perpetrators. That raises the question "When horrific acts of violence are intentionally committed, are forgiveness and reconciliation necessary or even good?" What does forgiveness really mean? Is it a necessary part of reconciliation? Is reconciliation a necessary part of forgiveness? Are the two even related and necessary for the other? Can you forgive and forget, forgive and never forget? Can either be demanded? If forgiveness is saved for the serious stuff—you don't forgive someone for a minor incident—is there ever a time when the serious stuff is beyond forgiveness?

WHAT'S FORGIVENESS GOT TO DO WITH IT?

> I forgive, but I remember. I do not forget the pain, the loneliness, the ache, the terrible injustice. But I do not remember it to inflict guilt or some future retribution. Having forgiven, I am liberated. I need no longer be determined by the past. I move into the future free to imagine new possibilities.
> —FATHER MARTIN LAWRENCE JENCO, *BOUND TO FORGIVE*

On January 8, 1985, Father Marty Jenco was kidnapped on the streets of Beirut, Lebanon, and was held hostage until July 16, 1986. His captivity was a journey of chaos, loss, hope, and healing for himself and for all of those who were his friends. After his release and while he was writing his book, we spent many hours together discussing what forgiveness meant to each of us.

We both agreed that forgiveness is not a verb, nor is it an act of the will. Forgiveness is the voice of the heart that speaks in the presence of the soul. It is heart business—the mind will be busy enough working out ways to demonstrate the forgiveness: through feelings, deeds, actions, possibly releasing debt, and making real other tangible expressions of that forgiveness.

As Marty said, "I am liberated. I need no longer be determined by the past. I move into the future free to imagine new possibilities." His forgiveness did not require that those who tortured him confess, repent, or make restitution. That would again hold him hostage to those who were intentionally cruel to him. In fact, the forgiveness was not about them. It was an act of "radical self-interest" in which he now had a sense that he need not thirst for revenge or bear ill will against the men who had tortured him; his life from that point on would not be *defined* by his captivity and torture; and he opened a way in himself for new beginnings that might—but might not necessarily—involve the possibility of reconciliation with those who tortured him. They would have plenty of heart, mind, and physical work to do before they could even approach him to reconcile.

The key here is that reconciliation was not necessary for Marty to be liberated. Which raises again the question: What is forgiveness? When Marty discussed forgiveness, notice that he did not mention the people who harmed him. It wasn't something he did *for* any other person. Rather it was his heart's decision not to be bound up in revenge and hatred. If there was any action in the word, it was in releasing himself from what he called "eating the silage of bitterness and resentment." His mind and heart had a few battles of their own, along with some mighty passionate discussions with his fellow hostages over forgiveness, vengeance, and revenge. Deep caring once again trumped everything else.

He talked about the many times during his captivity that he would, in his mind, circle down through Dante's rings of hell and remind himself of the first book of *The Divine Comedy*. In Canto XXXIII of the *Inferno*, Dante writes of two political allies who once lived in thirteenth-century Pisa, Archbishop Ruggieri degli Ubaldini and Count Ugolino della Gherardesca. Ultimately, the archbishop betrayed the count and sealed him and his sons and grandsons into a tower, where they eventually starved to death. During his pilgrimage through Hell, Dante finds the count and the archbishop frozen together in one hole, with the count, consumed with hatred, gnawing upon the archbishop's skull in his eternal hunger for vengeance.

For too long we have been taught that we must forgive those who have harmed us—especially when they *ask* for forgiveness. It doesn't seem to matter whether they are sincere or whether they are asking forgiveness to get their own relief from guilt, to get out of a longer prison sentence, or in the case of Wiesenthal's dying soldier, to "avoid the fires of Hell." In April 2004 at the ceremony in Kigali, Rwanda, marking the ten-year anniversary of the genocide, one of those who were asked to speak to the crowd assured all of those who had asked for forgiveness for their crimes in the genocide that they would be forgiven and would "sit at the right hand of God." Those who refused to forgive the *génocidaires* for killing their children in front of them, butchering their kin, for hunting them like animals, would find themselves "burning in Hell" for refusing to forgive. Wow! Is that message messed up! Let's heap more burden on those already overburdened with nightmares and sorrow.

Answering Wiesenthal's question about forgiveness, Andre Stein wrote:

> Can we, indeed, advocate forgiveness toward those who have committed crimes against humanity?…
> The consequences of participating in genocidal acts must include dying with a guilty conscience.
> Such a warning could be meaningful to those teetering between good and evil and those who insinuate that survivors be nobler than they can afford to be. We must stop dictating moral postures to the survivors. The opposite of forgiving is neither cruelty nor wallowing. It is a way of healing and honoring our pain and grief.

Forgiveness is not something that can be demanded—and I'm suggesting here that perhaps it should not be sought. We don't usually go around asking people to give us a gift, or to demand a gift from them and still assume it can be called a gift. Forgiveness *is* a gift, and that gift is to *oneself*.

I'm also not so sure that the person who forgives can even will that forgiveness when it is demanded or requested. In these stories, it was not the talk of forgiveness that mattered as much as it was the idea of reaching out as "one caring." Marty reached out during his captivity to his captors with the compassion that was so much a part of who he was. His fear was that the torture would kill in him that which he held as his "caring self." John Maxwell spoke up for the release of the man who killed his son. Bud Welch welcomed into himself the grief felt by the father and sister of the man who killed his daughter, and in sympathy asked, "What are *you* going through?" He fought to keep Timothy McVeigh from being executed. Simon Wiesenthal brushed away flies from the dying soldier's head, and when he met the soldier's mother, "I kept silent rather than shatter her illusions about her dead son's inherent goodness." While she was still grieving herself, Mathilde Rathenau reached out to the mother of her son's killer.

Perhaps what is important for our children is not that they be asked to learn to forgive someone else, but that we help them to hold on to their "caring self." And if we must use the word "forgiveness," we understand that the act of forgiveness is an act of "radical self-interest." When they have been grievously harmed, I will not ask them to forgive the one who harmed them, but I will ask them to be open to life again, to learn to trust again, and to treat all whom they meet with integrity, civility, and compassion. They do not have to like the person who has harmed them; they don't have to be their friend. We as parents have to say to the child who has been targeted in any way:

1. I hear you. I am here for you. I believe you.
2. You are not in this alone.
3. You did nothing to cause this.
4. There are things you can do.

The person who has caused such grievous harm will need to stand humbled (not humiliated); to take full responsibility for his actions (no excuses or blame-shifting); to present what he is going to do to keep it from ever happening again; to propose what he will do to make whatever restitution is possible; to ask the person(s) he harmed what they need to know about what he did; and finally be willing to listen to their story—if they want to tell it. He can offer his hand in reconciliation, but know that it might not be received. He, too, then must go on to "a life of new possibilities."

Reconciliatory justice is an act of healing in a community. It is perhaps the one tool that can begin to cut through the chains of violence. It does not excuse the violence, and it does not deny the dignity and worth of the victim or the humanity of the oppressor. It does justice to the suffering without perpetuating the hatred. It is the triumph of mindfulness and compassion over vengeance and retribution.

> We cannot live only for ourselves. A thousand fibers
> connect us with our fellow men; and among those
> fibers, as sympathetic threads, our actions run as
> causes, and they come back to us as effects.
> —HERMAN MELVILLE

Epilogue: Creating a Caring Community through Our Human Wisdom

It is not that humans are merely capable of acting beyond narrow self-interest. Rather, it's that we all have within us a need to do exactly that…. Through service to others, we affirm—for ourselves as well as for those we serve—another, truer way of looking at the world than from a perspective contorted by hate and fear and even grief…. So I can tell you with absolute certainty that the need so many feel to seek a meaningful purpose for their lives and to join in supportive communities is no aberration.

—ROBERT A WATSON, "ALTRUISM JUST FEELS RIGHT," *USA TODAY*

Raising kids who can think and act ethically involves nurturing their innate need to act "beyond narrow self-interest"; to care deeply, share generously, and help willingly; to stand up for another child and against an injustice. At the same time, it involves creating peaceful and just homes, schools, and communities that will effectively support us in parenting our kids. That means finding ways of being in the world that will reduce the harm we do to one another and to our planet.

In an attempt to better understand how this can be accomplished, I have over the last thirty-six years studied parenting—both the "book learning" type and the hands-on experience of raising my three children. I have also learned invaluable lessons from all of the parents and children I have met in my work. I know there are no quick fixes or easy solutions and no owner's manual that will give all the answers. Nor is it possible to pour into our children all we have learned. Their learning must come from the inside out. They need opportunities to care and to share and to help. They need to be accountable for what they do or fail to do. They also need opportunities to reflect on moral issues, work through ethical dilemmas, and determine for themselves what kind of people they would like to become.

During the last fifteen years I have studied genocide—the annihilation of family and community. I wanted to explore what in our dispositions and situations could possibly allow such evil to be perpetrated by one person—without shame, compassion, or mercy—and grievously suffered by another. I was also interested in the makeup of people who are willing to speak out against injustices or risk their own lives to rescue those whom their neighbors were out to destroy.

Regarding the first issue, what keeps coming up over and over is that genocide happens in an environment that is the antithesis of one created by a Backbone family. A genocidal environment consists of unquestioning obedience to authority, the normalization of cruelty, and the dehumanization of people. Hate—often the cold hate of contempt—is a key ingredient. Couple that hate with hoarding and harming, and you have a recipe for the destruction of a family, the demise of a community, or the annihilation of an entire group of people. These three virulent agents rip apart the fabric of human relationships. Hate destroys the "Thou," rendering the other an "It." Hoarding, with its rapacious and exploitive individualism, blinds us to the needs of others and to their rightful place in a genuine community. Harming—lying, cheating, and stealing—violates the critical bonds of trust.

There is no "I" without a "Thou," no "We" without community, and no way to survive without honoring both our unique individuality and our common humanity. We can no longer view hatred as natural, normal, or necessary; disparity in wealth as inevitable; or injustice as simply regrettable.

Father George Zabelka was the Catholic chaplain for the 509th Composite Group, a unit organized and trained specifically to drop the atomic bombs on Japan during World War II. Deeply troubled by his complicity and silence years after the bombs were dropped, Father Zabelka wrote, "To fail to speak to the utter moral corruption of the mass destruction of civilians was to fail as a Christian and as a priest. Hiroshima and Nagasaki happened in and to a world and a Christian church that had asked for it—that had prepared the moral consciousness of humanity to do and to justify the unthinkable."

Fifty years later, much of the world community turned a blind eye to the genocide in Rwanda. General Roméo Dallaire wrote of how, with silent indifference, the international community endorsed "the ethical and moral mistake of ranking some humans as more human than others." And according to Stephen Lewis, the United Nations' special envoy for HIV/AIDS in Africa, that continent is in a race against time in terms of the AIDS pandemic. Crossing Canada to deliver the 2005 Massey Lectures on this subject, Lewis said he wanted to speak "for all those little girls and all those mothers whose lives have been torn from their moorings, and whose future is in the hands, at least in part, of those who have always pretended to care, and have never really cared."

To do and to justify the unthinkable, to rank some humans as more human than others, and to pretend to care and never really care is to deny our common humanity. It was with a heavy heart and troubled mind that I, as a former Franciscan nun, studied the complicity of religions in so many wars, in all of the genocides, and in the failure to stem the tide of AIDS. Such complicity was omitted from the history books I studied in high school and was barely touched upon in university texts—and those writings were often one-sided and biased. Raul Hilberg, the distinguished Holocaust historian, wrote, "There are some things that can be done only so long as they are not discussed, for once they are discussed they can no longer be done." It is time for discussion in our homes, our schools, and our communities—and as a world community—about the complicity of religion in hate crimes and crimes against humanity, about indifference, about apathy, and about our moral consciousness.

I have come to the realization that religion is neither sufficient nor necessary to raise a moral child—a child who cares deeply, shares generously, and helps willingly, who refuses to hate, to hoard, or to harm. When asked about his beliefs, the renowned war photographer James Nachtwey answered, "I do not put my faith in God or divine intervention. I put my hope in humanity because all we have is each other." Nachtwey, who has witnessed some of the most horrific acts of violence committed against children and photographed that mayhem in hopes of shattering our collective indifference to the horrors of war, still puts his hope in humanity. Can those of us who have witnessed far less not do the same?

For many of the individuals who did speak out or who risked their own lives to rescue others, religion played a minor role, if any, in their decision to act. Many saw what they did as a *must*, not because it was their duty or obligation or because they felt bound by their religious tenets. In fact, many had no professed religion, and some acted in direct opposition to their church leaders and church dogma.

Can religion be harmful? Yes, in as much as it serves to divide us. In as much as it serves to give some people a sense of entitlement, a liberty to exclude, and intolerance toward differences. In as much as it denies equal rights and partnership between men and women. In as much as it fails to support a just economic order and basic human rights.

Can religion be helpful? Yes, in as much as it helps children to honor the "I and Thou" and the "We." In as much as it validates the intrinsic dignity of each human being and affirms our solidarity and our interdependence. In as much as it provides rituals and ethical traditions that help us develop our authentic selves in relation to a genuine community.

This book is about an ethic rooted not in principles, rules, customs, or dogma, but in deep caring: caring deeply for our own children and our neighbors' children and nurturing their innate ability to care, helping them to see themselves as both lovable and loving. Can we wish others abundant joy and a quiet peace? Can we show a deep passion to alleviate another's pain and sorrow and let that become part of our everyday life? Can we reach out to our neighbors who are suffering their own personal tragedies and ask, "What are you going through?" "What do you need?" "What can I do?" Can we be there for them as they name their loss, honor their grief, confront their pain, and tell their story? Can we also rejoice in their joys, their accomplishments, and their gains? Can we wish them enough, as we take only what we need? This is the human wisdom that enables us to meet one another morally. When we respond with a generous spirit, discernment, and mercy, when we help to alleviate the suffering of others and offer them our compassion and loving-kindness, we create caring communities and safe harbor for our children.

> There is nothing so like anything else as we are to one another ... the whole foundation of the human community consists in the links between person and person, whether foreigner or member of one's own family, and these links are kindness, generosity, goodness, and justice.
>
> —CICERO, *ON LAW*

Acknowledgments

My heartfelt thanks to:

Cynthia Good, former publisher of Penguin Group (Canada), for floating the idea of an ethics book when you accepted my first book, *kids are worth it!*, then asking once again two years ago, trusting that the time was right and that I could write it.

Barbara Berson, senior editor at Penguin Group (Canada), for your keen eye, probing questions, and ability as consummate taskmaster. I am grateful for your patience, support, and friendship through this writing project. Your editing expertise has transformed my ramblings into a coherent book.

David Davidar, current publisher of Penguin Group (Canada), for your patience and understanding and for giving me the time to get this book right.

Catherine Marjoribanks, for your attention to detail, consistency, and structure—all of which I tend to lose when translating my lectures into writing. Thanks for finding them and helping to make this book an easy read.

Patrick Crean, my literary agent, for listening to me rant and rave once again about never ever writing another book and then being there with your wisdom, knowledge, humor, and philosophical discussions every step of the way through this writing adventure.

Sandra Tooze, for orchestrating the production of the book and bringing together such talented people as proofreaders Maryan Gibson and Tara Tovell, and formatter Christine Gambin. Amazing!

Linda Ingram, my friend and neighbor, for helping me with the research and even more for the conversations about ethics over tea. I am grateful for your friendship, caring, insight, and cell phone calls to check up on my sanity as this book was nearing the end.

Satomi Morii, for keeping our office and my schedule in some semblance of order these last two years, but most of all for your friendship.

Sally Hauck, my friend and colleague, for sharing the many articles about ethics and teenagers. Your calls and notes of support helped keep me going.

The authors I have quoted throughout this book, whose writings have greatly influenced my work.

My three grown children, Anna, Maria, and Joseph, for your love, encouragement, and daily presence through phone calls, e-mails, and quick visits, and all those ethical issues you continue to raise.

Don, for introducing me to George Lakoff's books, all the articles and columns you came across to support or refute my writings, and the reassurance you gave our kids that these ethical issues I asked them about were the same ones I brought up during our university days to torment our professors. Yes, Martin Buber was right: Kant was mistaken.

Stephen Lewis, the United Nations' special envoy for HIV/AIDS in Africa, for your contagious passion and compassion. I cherish our friendship. The Stephen Lewis Foundation (www.stephenlewisfoundation.org) has given many of us a way to care more deeply, share more generously, and help more willingly.

You, the reader. By purchasing this book you have made the life of a child in Africa a little bit better. Thank you for caring.

Index